'This book is full of wise and p~~ractical~~ ~~~~ the very unique environment of ministry life. Having these tips is like having a wise counsellor journey with you through your children's most formative years, with the goal of keeping strong connections with you and with God.'
Lt Colonel Naomi Kelly, assistant principal for ministry development, Eastern Territory, College for Officer Training, Salvation Army

'What I value greatly in Rachel Turner's book is how she doesn't avoid the "tricky bits"; she tackles them head on through sharing real stories that add an authentic edge as she suggests alternative habits for us to form. This book is the work of someone who knows the reality and challenges of being both a parent and a church leader. And it overflows with understanding and helpful approaches that enable us to parent well. *Parenting as a Church Leader* is a book that will enable everyone in these unique roles – as well as their children – to grow and fully flourish.'
Gail Adcock, family ministries development officer, Methodist Church

'If the first church that we lead is the one at home, most of us in full-time paid ministry need a lot more training. I am grateful to Rachel for helping us parent well when it often feels that we face unique pressures as families in the context of church leadership.'
Paul Harcourt, national leader, New Wine England

The Bible Reading Fellowship
15 The Chambers, Vineyard
Abingdon OX14 3FE
brf.org.uk

The Bible Reading Fellowship (BRF) is a Registered Charity (233280)

ISBN 978 0 85746 937 3
First published 2020
10 9 8 7 6 5 4 3 2 1 0
All rights reserved

Text by Rachel Turner 2020
This edition © The Bible Reading Fellowship 2020
Cover illustration by Rebecca J Hall

The author asserts the moral right to be identified as the author of this work

Acknowledgements
Scripture quotations are taken from The Holy Bible, New International Version
(Anglicised edition) copyright © 1979, 1984, 2011 by Biblica. Used by permission of
Hodder & Stoughton Publishers, a Hachette UK company. All rights reserved. 'NIV'
is a registered trademark of Biblica. UK trademark number 1448790.

Scripture quotations marked CEV are taken from the Contemporary English
Version of the Bible published by HarperCollins Publishers, copyright © 1991,
1992, 1995 American Bible Society.

Every effort has been made to trace and contact copyright owners for material
used in this resource. We apologise for any inadvertent omissions or errors, and
would ask those concerned to contact us so that full acknowledgement can be
made in the future.

A catalogue record for this book is available from the British Library

Printed and bound by CPI Group (UK) Ltd, Croydon CR0 4YY

Rachel Turner

Parenting as a Church Leader

Helping your family thrive

Contents

PART IV: EMPOWERED

Introduction

Parenting as a church leader brings extraordinary complexity to the very tough job of parenting. We are trying to raise our children in what feels like a goldfish bowl, with an expectant congregation watching how we lead, how we parent and how our children feel and behave. We feel intensely the contrasting pulls of the church's needs on one side and our family's needs on the other, like the rope in a tug of war. The boundary between work and home blends together, as our families are present in our workplace and our workplace spills over into our homes. And, as hard as it is for us, we are aware that it may be even more difficult for our children.

As church leaders we know that our connection with God, our individual life choices, our purpose and our personal relationships all get mushed together. We have a hard time separating where one begins and another ends. Our children run into the same problem, because so much of their life exists in relation to the church: their friendships, their time requirements and their family dynamics. For them, church, faith and how they feel about God get mushed together into one big experience.

We are so aware that our children's feelings about God can get messily entwined with how they feel about church and our job. We can see the stresses our leadership puts on us and the stresses it puts on our children. We can easily become afraid when we hear stories of other church leaders' children going off the rails and wonder what impact having a church leader as a parent is going to have on our children's futures. At the bottom of it all, the question of 'How will my church leadership affect my children's relationship with God and the church?' can niggle at our hearts.

It is commonly believed that there is an inevitable cost to our children when we choose to be in church leadership, that a negative emotional or spiritual impact is a natural and unavoidable part of being church leaders' children.

I disagree. We as parents have great power to shape *how* our children will experience the complex situations they live in. It is how we parent through those situations that makes all the difference.[1]

There are no guarantees for how our children's futures will turn out. They are on their own paths with God and will make their own choices. But while being raised in a church leader's home has its difficulties, it is also a fantastic place to be. Our children have access to boundless opportunities spiritually and emotionally because of their proximity to the church. If we can learn to parent our children through the complexities of church leadership, then we can position them as best we can to thrive now and in the future. When we do this well, our children can:

- know that we trust them to go on their own adventure with God and that we will cheer them on as they do
- be empowered and encouraged to discover daily what life with God looks like for them
- spread their wings to play the part they feel called to in the body of Christ
- feel the strength and joy of being an ordinary member of a congregation, able to make mistakes and be lifted up by others.

Four constants our children need from us

When I set out to write this book, I read every denominational report, every book I could get my hands on and every research paper and PhD dissertation I could find.[2] I conducted interviews and focus groups and ran pilot training days around the country. What

I discovered was this: there are four main constants our children need to feel in order to thrive as children of church leaders. If we can focus as parents on helping our children feel these four constants, then we can position them to thrive spiritually, mentally and emotionally now and in the future. Our children need to feel:

1 connected to us
2 prioritised by us
3 covered by us
4 empowered in their own faith journeys by us.

When our children feel *connected* to us, we are well set to proactively and powerfully encourage their faith. The more connected our children feel to us, the more likely they are to embrace what we embrace, including who God is and who he can be in their lives. Through connection flow our honest stories and authentic windows into our lives, which our children need to hear and see so they can begin to build their own path with God.

When our children feel *prioritised* by us, they can feel free to be themselves and feel valued within their family. We can ensure that they feel rooted in family first and therefore able to connect into the church because they see the church as a blessing rather than as the competition.

When our children feel *covered* by us, they feel free and able to build healthy relationships and connections with others, which will enable them to access the love, support and friendship of our congregations.

When our children feel *empowered* by us to go on their own faith journeys, they can be free to make their own faith choices. This empowerment enables them to own their personal connection with God, not for the sake of us as their parents, or as a performance for the congregation, but for themselves.

About this book

Parenting as a church leader can be isolating. It can be hard for us to find wisdom and people to parent alongside who understand the unique context we live in. This book exists to give you encouragement, hope and access to the wisdom and voices of other families who have walked, and are walking, the same path.

All the stories in this book are real, taken from interviews with church-leader families and stories told by participants in training days. The book is organised in four sections, covering the four constants our children need to experience to thrive in our ministry context. Each section starts with a description of the specific constant and then expands into ways you can apply it to your family and work life. Each section ends with a 'Tricky bits' chapter, which applies the constant to a specific scenario of ministry life.

For the sake of brevity, I often use the term 'our children' in the book. By this I mean children of all ages. The principles in this book are just as applicable to 20-year-olds as they are to three-year-olds; the difference is in how we implement the principles. It is never too early to begin implementing these ideas and, as we have seen over and over, it is never too late.

Before we begin, I want to thank you for your ministry. Church leadership is a wonderful, tough, joyous and exhausting call, and you have boldly stepped into it with your family. Your family *can* thrive in the middle of it all. Helping our children meet and know God is one of the greatest joys of parenting, and this book will help you find what it looks like for you.

There is no single right way for you to do this. Within this book, you will find information to help you think through the issues you face in your particular family scenarios and help you apply the concepts to your needs. We will cover all the quandaries of ministry life: parent vs leader tension, living in a goldfish bowl, the congregation's expectations and much more. God called you into ministry and life to the full, and he wants you and your children to flourish, not for an easy life but for a powerful, loved, effective life full of faith.

May God give you much peace and joy as you dive into exploring how you can help your family thrive as you lead.

I

Connected

1

The importance of connection

I've always wanted to go skydiving. I think it's about the adventure of leaping from the relative safety of a plane and out into the unknown, becoming completely helpless, and then falling, zooming, down through the rushing air. Oh, the thrill! My plan is to go tandem the first time, attached to an experienced skydiver, like one of those babies in a front-facing baby carrier. The skydiver would be the one responsible for knowing how high we were, for checking all the equipment, for deploying the chute at the right time and for getting us safely down to our landing site. I'd have total trust in the experienced skydiver. My only worry, though, would be about the strength of the equipment that would attach me to her! What if our chute deployed and I kept falling? Before I'd jump, I'd want to know that my skydiver made sure our connection together would be 100% safe and secure. This connection would be the best safety feature I'd have.

It's the same for our children.

For us, ministry life can feel like a wonderful adventure, full of incredible moments, hard work, great thrills and tough seasons. As we go along, we bring our ability to deal with the emotions of leadership and ministry life to bear on our situations. Ministry life has a steep learning curve, but it's the job we signed up for and we can navigate it well, given all our life experience and training.

But we didn't just jump out into our ministry skydive alone, leaving our families behind. Our children are on this adventure with us. They don't have the experience and skills to navigate ministry life, but we do. It's our job to pull them close, to coach them through it and to pay attention to our connection to them. We need this important connection to be solid, in order to coach our children and to keep them safe so that they can enjoy the ride.

Many parents deeply love their children, but they don't know how to build a deep connection with them. Connection is more than love and affection. It's about relationality. It's about feeling seen, loved and understood. It's about feeling unconditionally loved, heard and valued. This sense of connection is what makes us feel safe in our relationships with our friends and family. Connection is what enables us to feel loved, to be willing to change, to be encouraged, to be corrected and to receive wisdom and ministry. Connection is the essence of relationship. If we are going to go ministry skydiving with our children, we must pay attention to developing this connection. Because without it, our children are untethered and skydiving alone.

Research repeatedly shows how important this connection is. Care for the Family did a study on parents helping their children find faith,[3] and they found that one of the significant factors for children finding their own faith was the strength of their connection to their Christian parents. Martin Weber, in his PhD research on clergy children's attrition from faith,[4] noted that a lack of relational connection was one of the main factors behind clergy children rejecting faith.

The disconnection of swapping hats

One of the main factors that leads to our lack of connection with our children is our sense of being torn between two roles – our church leader role and our parent role – as if we are endlessly swapping hats.

We wear our church leader hat when we are required to focus on the needs and discipling of our congregants, the development of our teams, the shaping of our next sermon, the rolling out of the church strategy, and all the events and little bits we catch. We can be in the flow, leading the church with full focus. Our congregants assume we wear this hat most of the time, so when they see us out and about, they assume we are 'on duty', ready to respond to them.

We wear our parent hat when we put our family at the centre of our focus. We come home from work, mentally take off our ministry hat and put on our parent hat, and sit down and play with the kids. When our children see us, they assume we are wearing our parent hat and are 'on duty' as their parent, ready to respond to them.

Unfortunately, ministry life isn't just 9-to-5. While other people get to go home and firmly put on their parent hat, we can't. Our home time looks a bit different. For example, you may be relaxing at home after work, listening to your child talk about 'Roman day' at school, when the phone rings. It's the church administrator. You think, 'No, I'm wearing my parent hat,' and you ignore the call, patting yourself on the back. Then the phone rings again, and it's the same number. 'Argh,' you think. 'It may be important.' With an apologetic look at your child, you say, 'Hang on a minute. I'll be right back.' You swap your parent hat for your church leader hat and take the phone call, which leads to a quick set of emails. You finish your work and then swap back to your parent hat for tea, and then whack on that church leader hat once again to quickly prep for the evening's budget meeting, before you throw the parent hat back on for bedtime kisses, and finally place the church leader hat on for the last time as you head out the door.

And that's not even talking about a Sunday morning or a meeting at your house when your children *and* the congregation are present together – in the same place at the same time – and *each* group expects you to be continually wearing the hat that signals to them that you are 'on duty' and ready to respond.

Whether you're trying to remove a child who has attached herself to you when you're leading the service, or you're struggling with your teenager slumped in the front row rolling his eyes at you, the stress can be enormous. You may try to look at your children and signal, 'Can't you see my hat? I have my church leader hat on right now. This is not parent hat time!' But it appears that your children *cannot see* your invisible church leader hat.

This pattern of swapping hats can be a source of enormous confusion for our children, and it can create a disconnection in our relationship with them. Whether or not we are in a church leader situation, our children are communicating to us, 'I love you and I need you to love me, care for me, make me safe and encourage me. I need you to parent me.' When we swap into our church leader hat, we are effectively telling our children, 'I am *not* your parent right now. I'm here for the congregation. I'm here for everyone else in this room *but* you.' Our children can feel the force of that rejection and can react to that message. For them, church events can become a process of managing how much disconnection they can handle before they think, 'Wait a minute. I can make you put your parent hat back on. Watch this!' And then they demonstrate with their behaviour how quickly they can force us to be a parent again. Behaviour often becomes a way for children to force us to put the parent hat back on. Ever wonder why it feels like sometimes our children's behaviour gets worse at the most inopportune times – before meetings, during sermons, after church services? Sometimes it's about our children fighting to get their parent back.

But we don't have to live in that struggle. We can have an integrated life, holding close our ministry and our family, honouring them both at the same time. I believe that when God calls us to be church leaders *and* parents, it is one call, not two. It is one hat, not two. At the heart of living with one call, of wearing one hat, is how we develop and maintain connection with our children so that we can say, 'I'm your parent all the time, and this is what it looks like for us to stay connected right now as I lead.'

So what *does* that look like? When we are connected to our children, and our children feel connected to us, then the following can happen:

- We will be positioned to influence and help them in their journey with God.
- We can have the heart-to-heart conversations that enable us to coach them through the complexities resulting from the ministry context in which they live.
- We can provide insight into the beauty of the church. We can explain and help our children see where God is in a community of broken, messy and wonderful people. We can help them see life through our eyes and God's eyes.
- We can help our children make sense of the nature of God's calling and how we are trying to be faithful to it.
- We will be laying a foundation for a relationship with them now, as well as for one in the future.

It can be so easy to lose sight of this concept of connection, particularly with the schedule of ministry life. Our days can be unpredictable and packed with activities and the responsibility of meeting a variety of needs. Emails, meetings, one last phone call or last-minute prep can mean that family connection gets robbed, replaced with merely being together in the same room and getting through the activities of the day.

The solution to this difficulty isn't to simply 'be home more'; it is to create a pattern and habit of connecting with each other in our time together. Connection, then, is the glue that keeps families close and communication flowing. If we don't proactively build and maintain connection, we will begin to lose our ability to help our children flourish.

If ministry life isn't about frantically switching hats, we can find a way to hold and honour both our ministry and our family. Connection with our children becomes something vital that we can build, maintain and grow in the midst of still doing our job well.

How do we build connection?

The good news is that we already know how to build and maintain connection with our friends and family. All we need to do is proactively apply those concepts to our children.

Take a moment to think about the people in your life with whom you feel connected. Consider your relationships with your friends, siblings or even parents. In your experience with relationships, what are the ways in which you feel connected to your friends? To your family? How do you build and sustain those connections?

It may be that you:

- laugh together
- invest in time together: scheduled time and bored-togetherness time
- share interests and memories
- share important things of the heart back and forth
- are able to be open and honest
- encourage and support and see your words make a difference
- feel listened to and love listening to them
- access their understanding and empathy
- feel they are not judging you
- depend on their faithfulness and know they will show up or answer the phone when you need them
- walk together through good times and bad times
- share a mutual trust built on years of faithfulness and work.

Building connection happens in the everyday moments of faithfulness, expressions of love, listening, laughing, honesty, mutual joy and memories.

This type of connection is the essence of family life. It can happen in times of boredom or incredible significance, in sharing hearts and laughter, through little things and big things. These opportunities to build connection are everywhere, at home and at church. Some opportunities require time, but others just require a choice.

The unique situation we find ourselves in as church leaders is that we are around our children while we are both at home and at work. If we want our children to flourish, then we need to find a way to create a thread of connection throughout all the time we are around them, not just during our time at home. Don't worry – it's easier than you think; the opportunities are all around if we look for them.

Create a language

There was a time in my life when I was very ill and my brain wouldn't work properly. I couldn't remember the words for what I wanted to communicate. I'd be thirsty and would ask my husband to please get me a… *what was it called*? I was desperate to be understood. I'd act it out. I'd describe it as a 'make-my-mouth-stop-being-sticky thing'. I'd point repeatedly. I would try so hard to communicate my one deep desire to have a drink. Without specific words to rely on, I felt powerless to communicate my needs.

In our relationship with our children, they can find it hard to communicate with us about connection, primarily because they don't have a language for it. They can feel connected or disconnected, but their feeling is simply a sense or fleeting emotion that they cannot articulate. If they don't have the vocabulary and experience, they couldn't say, for instance, 'When you have four evening meetings in your week, I begin to feel a bit disconnected from you because we don't have our before-bed giggle time, so I feel like I never laugh with you.' Instead, all they have to use are a lot of desperate behaviours to express the sense of what they may be feeling. They may act out, using poor choices so that you have to spend time with them to discipline them. They may pretend not to want to be around you and punish you by shutting you out. They may be very positive on the outside, but just feel an internal sense of grief or of floating away, so they share less with you or expect less support. Their behaviour becomes their communication method, which makes it hard for us to understand them and reconnect.

If our children don't have a language for what they are feeling, they won't know how to communicate that feeling to us and they won't have a pathway towards understanding that feeling for themselves. A recent study showed not only the power of connection between parents and children, and all the good it brings, but also that it's in the power of connection that the child feels rather than the parent.[5] In other words, whether or not we feel connected to our children seems to be much less important than how connected our children feel to us. If we are going to help our children grow this connection with us and flourish in it, then we must first give them a language to use to describe and process their feelings and to help them understand and know that we are on their side.

I would suggest that you talk with your children about connection in ways that flow from your everyday life with them. Through whatever language you choose to use – 'feeling like a together family', 'velcroed together', 'hearts like Lego bricks locked in', 'arm in arm vs floating down the river alone' or simply 'having our hearts connected' – children and teens need to learn what the goals of connection are all about.

Help children and teens identify when they are and aren't feeling connected by naming it

One of our jobs with children is to help them name their emotions and experiences. When we have toddlers and we see them experiencing emotions, it's our job to explain to them what is happening: 'It looks like you are feeling angry' or 'What a happy time we are having!' By naming their emotional experiences, our children can begin to understand and cope with them.

But what if we never had a word for anger or regret, sadness or happiness? We'd be experiencing something without being able to talk about it. It would be incredibly frustrating for our children and for us. If our children are on a journey of connection with us, they need a language they can use to discuss their connection with us and to reflect upon this connection themselves, using specific words to describe when it's not working and when it is. One way to start is to name the emotional experience when it is happening: for example, 'I love hugs. I feel like my heart and your heart are connected when we hug'; or, after a tickle fest, finish by saying, 'Laughing together is one of the best things in my life. Our hearts feel locked together in joy when we laugh.' I know others who name an experience by saying:

> Is there anything that you are worried about that may mean your heart is hiding from me a bit? I feel like a bit of you isn't letting me come close, like a piece of Velcro that can't quite get a grip because it's covered with carpet fluff. I feel our hearts are missing connecting with each other. How can I help with that?

For teenagers and older children, you might want to start by saying:

> It is so important to me that you feel seen, heard and loved, that you feel that you can say anything to me and that we feel that nothing is building up between us. I want us to feel connected, in whatever way that looks right for us. I may start asking about how our connection is doing and if you ever feel disconnected from me. That's just me asking if there is anything we could do better to make sure that our relationship is the best it can be, because I love you so much.

Use the language to monitor how everyone is feeling and work as a team to problem-solve

Mutual problem-solving means that everyone in the family is working towards staying connected as a team. By giving a language in which to discuss the problem, the whole family then can work to solve it. For instance, a goal might be to say, 'I know it's Christmas, and that means my work schedule gets crazy. I want to make sure that we don't just get time together, but that we stay heart-to-heart connected. So let's make a plan for our busy weeks. What patterns do we need to put in place to help us stay connected?' Or you could say, 'Hey, I've felt like we've had a bit of a bump in our connection. What can I do differently to help us reconnect better?'

You might also say, 'Sometimes I don't see you at all and I think we are missing out on some really peaceful times together before you go to school. Will you experiment with me to see if I can help make our connection better? I thought this week I will try to sit down at the breakfast table for 20 minutes every morning, no phone, ready to laugh and talk with everyone.' Or you might say, 'Okay, last week it looked like you struggled with me when I was not able to give you my time and my face. What can we try this week that might work for you and for me?'

This language helps children and teens identify what they are feeling, which then allows each family member to proactively work on building and maintaining connection together, and it also allows the entire family, as a team, to problem solve for ways to stay connected.

We are on a grand adventure of ministry. Let's make sure that our children are connected into us so that they can flourish while on this adventure. In the next chapter we will be talking about how we can practically build connection with our children and teens in the midst of ministry.

2

Growing connection in the midst of ministry

It is important for us to create moments when we can *deliberately* connect with our children. These special moments will help remind us and our children that we are connected, and they will assure our children of the love and emotional closeness we have with them, no matter what we are doing.

Creating these moments, these emotional connection points, doesn't take a lot of time and isn't burdensome. With some initial planning, they can become simple and quick approaches that will ensure that our continued connection with our children remains strong.

These emotional connection points should be practical and simple to use *in the midst of* our everyday church work, as well as in our homes; we can use them when we are with our children and when we are apart from them.

Gary Chapman and Ross Campbell's concept of love languages helps with this approach. In their book *The 5 Love Languages of Your Family*[6] they discuss that people, including children, tend to perceive love in five different ways. They say that *all of us* have *all of these* love languages within us, but each of us tends to significantly lean towards one or two of them.

The five main love languages are:

- *Quality time* – Children with this love language want to be with those they love. They enjoy their company, and they want to share together in life and important moments. These are the kids who like to have one-to-one time with you and who repeatedly ask you to play with them when you're writing a sermon. They want your attention. These are the children who may be full of things to tell you, during the service, after church and at home.

- *Touch* – Children with this love language feel close through touching. They love hugs and back scratches, holding hands and sitting close by your side. Younger ones love being held and attaching themselves to one of your limbs. Older teenagers tend to be the ones who lean on you or fling their legs over you when you sit nearby. At church, these children can become limpets, wanting to be held or wanting to stand with their arms wrapped around your leg while you lead the service.

- *Acts of service* – Children with this love language feel loved when you do things for them. Sometimes it can be annoying because they will ask you to do things that they are perfectly capable of doing themselves. These are the children who slow you down on a Sunday morning because they want you to buckle their shoe, even though they can buckle it themselves. They may want you to carry their bag or to pour squash for them during refreshments set-up before the service.

- *Gifts* – Children with this love language feel connected through gifts. They want you to give them stuff or bring them things. It is easy to think that these children are selfish or that they long for material things, but actually their desire is more rooted in wanting to be remembered by you when the two of you are apart. A gift tells them that when you were away, you looked at something and thought, 'My child would like that.'

- *Words of affirmation* – Children with this love language flourish with your words. They come alive when you compliment them, and they sparkle when you speak positively to them. They are the ones who want to tell you a story about something great they did or who pester you after church or school to show you what they made so you can say, 'Wow! That's fantastic!' They love your encouragement and words.

Now take a moment and think about your children. Which love languages do you see them using? You can use your reflections as a guide for creating your own connection points with your children. Remember, connection is more than expressing affection; it's building relationships through togetherness, authentic sharing and love expressed well.

You don't need to connect non-stop; just create little points of connection in those times when your children are present, and you are in the midst of ministering and parenting at the same time. The following are examples from church leaders who have created their own connections.

Quality time

Quality time children want to be with you, so it's helpful to invest time in being with them and near them.

'My six-year-old loves coming with me early on a Sunday to hang out in my office, to help me set up for the service and Communion and to stand next to me while I lead the pre-service worship. In order to make this connection work well, I decided to add in an extra 15 minutes to my morning church routine. Now I'm a bit more peaceful during our slow walks to church. Her coming with me in the morning gives us some together time as we walk, and it gives us more side-by-side opportunities as we do things together before the service.'

* * *

'I found that bedtimes weren't working as connection time for our family because of all our evening meetings, so we began making morning breakfast time our main connection point. It has worked so much better for us to start the day catching up on our week and sharing feelings, laughter and thoughts. It's more connection than we ever had at night!'

* * *

'My son was two years old when he went through a season of severe clinginess. He would scream and scream, and every Sunday was a nightmare. One Sunday I just put a pillow and two bags of snacks at the bottom of the pulpit. When I went up to preach, my son just sat there, eating snacks and holding on to my leg. The congregation couldn't see him, and he was as good as gold. We spent a whole year with him eating through my 20-minute sermons.'

* * *

'We discovered the power of taking our children out to lunch. Since we controlled our schedules, we thought it would be a great together time. We picked a day during the week, and then every week one or both of us would show up to have lunch with one of our children. Sometimes we'd go out; other times it was a picnic in the car. Either way, it was a consistent time to talk.'

* * *

'Boring errands work best for me. Any time I have to do errands, I ask my *quality time* children to come with me. They love it, and I get stuff done!'

Extra skills for *quality time* children

When we have a child who values quality time, we often can feel that we say 'no' a lot to their repeated requests to do things with us. They want us to play or to take them out, and it can feel exhausting to reject them constantly. One of the concepts we want our children to know about God is that he longs to be with them, with us. He chooses a relationship with us, and he wants nothing to be between us and him. He seeks us out. He finds us. For a *quality time* child, this is an important concept we want them to grasp.

One tip for helping children who have a *quality time* love language is to use the 'play with me' approach every once in a while. It means the world to our children when we say to them, 'Play with me.' It communicates to them, 'I want to be with you. I want to play. Please be with me.' We might think it will be difficult to find the time, but it's not. It just takes a simple shift.

Think about the times when you are free and you know your child is going to ask you to play. Instead of waiting for them to ask, simply beat them to it. For example, on a Saturday morning, when you know your kid will soon wake up and ask you to play, don't wait. Thunder into their room, climb into their bed and say, 'Hey! I can't wait anymore. Wake up! Play with me!' You were going to be playing anyway. You might as well get up a bit early and overwhelm your child with your deep desire to be with them.

Another win/win is to ask your children to play with you when you know they will say no. Swing into the room when they have friends over and say, 'Hey, do you want to play with me?' They will roll their eyes and say, 'No, I'm busy,' and you can walk away as you hear your kids explain to their friends, 'She always wants to play with me.'

Sometimes you can set up a board game ahead of time, so it looks like you have spent all day looking forward to playing with them when they get home.

Whatever you choose to do, plan occasional, random times to show your children that you want to be with them and to play with them.

Words of affirmation

Children with this love language flourish with our words. When we find moments to affirm them in the midst of our ministry life, then our words can go a long way in helping them feel connected to us.

'My kids love little notes, so before the service I write something kind and positive on little sticky notes. When they leave for the children's groups, I stick them on their shirts somewhere, and they giggle and read them as they leave. Rather than getting grumpy, they look forward to going out now.'

* * *

'I make it a point to whisper to my children throughout the service, just checking on them. Whispering a quick, 'You okay? I love sitting with you,' goes a long way in helping my teen feel connected to me in the service.'

* * *

'Whenever I have an evening meeting at my house, I make sure that after all the coffees and welcomes, I excuse myself to run up to the children's bedroom for a minute. I quickly give each of them a kiss and tell them one thing I admire about them or am grateful for about them, or just something positive and affirming. I find that if I do this, then they come down the stairs a lot less often to ask me something. I realised that they were coming down because they wanted to have one last quick conversation and to get a final 'I love you'. Now I bring it to them without them needing to ask for it.'

* * *

'I was finding that sometimes I wouldn't see some of my kids in the morning before the service. We have an early 8.00 am service, so some days I'm there at 7.00 am to set up. It meant that the first time I saw them was when they were among the rest of the congregation, and it was causing some problems with our family feeling out of sorts and disconnected. Now, every once in a while when I'm on a train or bored waiting for a meeting, I write a quick note of affirmation to each of my children. Then I save them and post them under their doors on Saturday night, so if I don't see them on Sunday before the service (particularly my teens), then they wake up feeling connected to me even if I haven't seen them. Now on those Sundays, the children walk in feeling as if we have already made a morning connection.'

* * *

'Text messages have changed my relationship with my kids during evening meetings and services. If I'm away at an evening meeting, I'll text little messages, memes or gifs to my husband's phone for each kid. Then, as he's doing the bedtime routine, he can show each of the children a message I sent to them. For my 15-year-old, we have a private WhatsApp group, so I can send messages and silly photos to him when I'm away. I end up finding out much more info through these texts about what he's doing and feeling, which I can then bring up in conversation later.'

Extra skills for *words of affirmation* children

Connection isn't just expressing affection; it's also about creating a two-way bond. Children who have words of affirmation as a love language also tend to express their love in that way as well. One way to increase connection with these children is to create opportunities for them to encourage you. Feel free to come home at the end of the day and say, 'Phew, that was a tough day. Ever have a day when you think, "I have made so many mistakes"? Can you please tell me one thing I do that is good? That will make my heart strong again.' Then look your kid in the eye, hear their encouragement and say, 'Thank you so much for that. I needed your powerful words.' We feel connected to those whom we can help, so let's enable our *words of affirmation* kids to feel powerful in building connection too.

Touch

Sometimes it can feel like every child has this love language, but some children need more touch experiences than others. How can we connect with our children while still needing both our hands to do our jobs?

> 'I had a ten-month-old who refused to be put down, which was very awkward during a service. He screamed so much when I tried to hand him to my wife. I ended up preaching for months with him in a forward-facing baby carrier. He loved it, my congregation loved it and more dads started baby-wearing too. We had a mini dad-baby-wearing revolution at church due to my *touch* son.'

* * *

> 'I casually rub my daughter's shoulders throughout the worship, and she is as content as anything. At first I thought it might look a bit unprofessional, but it means that when worship is over, she no longer climbs on me or wants me to pick her up. I'm now able to focus on leading the service, and I can get up and down as needed.'

* * *

> 'We found that we were really struggling as a family because I sat on the chancel during the service. My children felt as if they weren't with me at church. I ended up choosing to change the way we did this, and I started sitting in the front row with my family. Now my two *touch* children can sit next to me and hold my hands as we go through the bits of the service they're in for. I feel like I had to change what I was displaying to the congregation. I changed from *I'm the powerful leader* to *I'm a father who is also a powerful leader.*'

* * *

'We discovered that I kept running out to evening meetings without saying a proper goodbye. I would just call out, 'Bye, see you later!' My *touch* kids struggled with that. I decided to make sure I started my exit five minutes earlier so I could sweep them up, look them in the eyes, pull them on my lap and snuggle a bit with kisses. This new pattern meant that they felt more connected to me, and my husband says they go to sleep with fewer arguments and behaviour problems.'

* * *

'My son used to want to fling himself on to me when he came back from kids' ministry. When I saw him approaching, I would actively block him and give him 'the look' as a warning, because I was usually in some deep conversation and didn't want him to interrupt. We talked about how we could feel more connected at church, and we came up with a plan that has been working. Now, I keep my hand behind my back at all times, and he can squeeze it any time he wants. And if he wants a hug, he can always feel free to slip in a squeeze around my waist, as long as he doesn't interrupt the conversation I'm having.'

* * *

'Assemblies at my daughter's school were becoming a problem until we both came up with a way to connect. She asked me to stand by the door with my hand by my side. Then when her class came in, we would both pretend not to know each other. At the last second, though, she would give me a low-down high five. It's a little sneaky touch connection that does not embarrass her, but still connects. We love it. She calls it *spy family*.'

* * *

'Working from home was hard for my *touch* children, so I began to tell them that they are welcome to pull up a chair next to me, or to ask me to sit on the couch next to them. I warned them that I will still need to stay focused on my work, but I would love to do my work next to them if they wanted. Now, my five-year-old will sometimes come in quietly with some colouring, pull up a chair and sit next to me, and colour with his little foot touching my leg. He may stay only five minutes, but it means so much. If my seven-year-old sees me reading, she asks if I can read on the couch, and then she gets her book, snuggles in under my arm and we have a great time snuggling and reading together.'

* * *

'I work from home, and we have 10.30 wrestle time. I have three children under five, and I think they are all *touch* children. At 10.30 every day, when I can manage it, we have a massive wrestle/tickle chase around the house for ten minutes. The kids are exhausted, as am I, but it means they happily ignore me for the rest of the day.'

Extra skills for *touch* children

Touch children often express their love through their hugs, touches and strong squeezes. They can sometimes be too rough or too intense. How we get them off us is important or else they can feel rejected. Using our words to affirm their expression of love is helpful, such as, 'Oh, thank you for that hug. It makes me feel so cared for,' or, 'That was such a gentle kiss on my head. Thank you!'

When your child is too exuberant and goes in for a face-squeeze or a neck-hug that is too tight, rather than getting angry give them some guidance on how that makes you feel: 'No, thank you. Hugs usually make me feel loved and safe, but this one is too rough for me. Please let go. I'm only up for gentle, kind hugs right now. Would you like to try a gentle hug?'

Acts of service

Acts of service children feel loved when we do things for them. Consequently, connecting with these children can feel a bit tricky because, as parents, we are naturally trying to get our children to learn to do things for themselves. It can be hard for us to strike a balance.

As church leaders, we often need our children to be able to just get on with things. We regularly feel we don't have the time or space in our ministry schedules to give anything extra to our *acts of service* kids. But there are ways we can. Here are a few examples of how some church leaders built connection with their *acts of service* children while being in the midst of ministry.

'Sunday mornings were like a nightmare. I'm a solo parent, so getting my two children dressed, fed and out the door was the most frustrating part of my morning. On a normal school day, I expect them to get themselves up, dressed and fed (they are 10 and 12). On Sundays, though, it's like they are moving through treacle. I end up yelling and ordering them around. It's not a great way to prep for ministry. I realised they both were *acts of service* children, and so I thought I'd try something new. I got up a bit early, set up the table and threw some pain au chocolat into the oven. I called for them to come down, kissed them on the head and told them I made them a special breakfast. As I continued to get ready, it felt like the whole morning shifted. I remembered that my youngest always gets thirsty at church, so I set out a water bottle for him by the front door. When it was time to go, I was able to say, 'It's time to go. I know how thirsty you guys get, so here are your water bottles ready to go. I'd hate for you to get thirsty at church. I am leaving in five!' It was the first time they were ready on time. As we left, they thanked me for breakfast and the water. It took me an extra five minutes in the morning, but the difference was huge. Now Sunday morning breakfast is a tradition they look forward to, and getting ready is no longer a problem.'

* * *

'We live a ten-minute walk away from the church. My children always asked me to drive, and I thought it was ridiculous. After discovering that all my family, including my wife, are *acts of service* people, I now make sure that if it is raining, I offer to drive. Rather than having a stressful, grumpy morning with the children, behaviour wise, it now turns out to be the best.'

* * *

'I have four teenagers, and they are fiercely independent, but two of them have strong *acts of service* needs. I find that offering to do things for them counts as actually doing things. If I offer to drive them someplace, then they feel loved, even if they don't want the ride. I make sure that during particular churchy times, when they might feel as if I'm not there for them, I up my acts of service. Whenever I'm making tea for any meeting in my house, I also make one for them and bring it to them with biscuits. Sometimes I do one of their chores for them when I'm taking a break from writing emails. All those little things add up to some great connection times. They used to complain about evening meetings in particular, but that has stopped since I started taking those quick moments to bring them tea and a little slice of whatever food or cake people brought!'

Extra skills for *acts of service* children

Children and teens who connect through acts of service also tend to demonstrate and express themselves through acts of service. It makes them feel connected to us when we notice what they do and when we make a big deal out of appreciating them. Their acts of service may be very small, and not necessarily something we would have thought we needed, but they are important to acknowledge.

From staying behind to pick up service sheets to putting all your shoes in a line at home or licking your bread because it 'looked too dry' (true story), our children are often expressing connection to us through their actions. When we meet their sacrifice and consideration with appreciation and love, we both feel a strength of connection. So keep your eyes open for all the small things your *acts of service* children may be doing for you, particularly if you are not naturally an *acts of service* person.

Gifts

We can be put off by children who have a *gifts* love language, as it may appear to us that they are becoming materialistic. We may respond negatively to their desires for us to give them things, particularly when, as church leaders, we don't have a lot of money. Over time, our *gifts* children can accidentally end up resenting the church for our lack of money, when their frustration is really about their love language being unmet.

One important point to remember is that gifts don't need to be expensive. Indeed, they don't even need to be bought. At the root of a *gifts* love language is the desire for someone they love to be thinking of them when they aren't together. While *quality time* people are all about being together, *gifts* people are about what you're thinking about when you're apart. Gifts can be little things, small tokens that say to your children, 'When I'm not with you, you are still in my heart and mind.' The constant back and forth of church ministry gives us plenty of opportunities to occasionally give gifts to our children.

'One day I was in the office, and a volunteer swung by and ended up making an incredibly fast paper aeroplane while he sat and talked. I had recently worked out that my daughter had a *gifts* love language, so I asked him if I could keep it, and I brought it home to show her. She responded as if I had bought her a million-pound diamond tiara. She's kept it for two years now, and it was just a paper aeroplane that would have gone in the bin. Now I just pick up stuff for her, like a big leaf, because I know she likes them. Anything really.'

* * *

'We have a lot of meetings in our house, and I have two children with a *gifts* love language. I found an easy win by only buying their favourite biscuits for my meetings. Whenever church people come around, my children are so excited because they know I will be shopping with them in mind.'

* * *

'If I have to go away for meetings or conferences, I leave for my kids one of those blank puzzles that you can get from craft shops. I just draw a picture or write a love message on it, and I leave it for them. They love it, and they can't wait to tell me all about making it. Now they make me puzzles, and we all look forward to connecting while we are away.'

Extra skill for *gifts* children

Children who have a *gifts* love language tend to shower us with gifts too. Generally, it is tat. Their gifts can be endless: half-coloured pieces of paper, a string from their pocket, a rock they thought was pretty. How we treasure them speaks volumes. To help your kid feel connected to you throughout your ministry time, make sure you use/keep/display/wear those things your kid gives you. Ugly pink tie? Wear it when you preach at the all-age service. Drawing of a half-monster-half-pizza? Tape it right up there by your computer in your office. Be very careful where you leave these gifts. I've heard of more than a few children who were crushed when they discovered their carefully created craft smashed under the couch or tossed in the bin. Many church leaders I know buy one of those nice-looking storage boxes, call it a memory box and use it to store all those precious gifts.

In summary, we are all dynamic, ever-changing human beings, and our growing children need to feel our love expressed through all these love languages. As seasons change, you will notice specific love languages becoming greater or less significant in your children's lives. Watch out for these shifts and ride the waves of what makes them feel most connected. As you continue to have your conversations with your children about connection, you will find it easy to creatively respond to what your children need next.

3

Tricky bits: coaching our children through the complexity of church

I remember my first trip to London. I was ten years old and so excited. This was back in the 1980s, before Oyster cards and Citymapper, when to navigate London you relied on signage, inner confidence and local knowledge. I was full of anticipation about experiencing everything in London, but especially travelling on the Underground.

When I entered the first Tube station with my parents, I was in awe of the swirl and speed of the bodies around me. People shot past us, and everyone seemed to know where they were going. They looked so cool, so assured, so focused on travel, and I wanted to be like them. I clung to my dad's hand, and my parents guided me to a big map on the wall. They found our location on the map and showed me where we were. Then they found the station we had to travel to. My mum traced our route with her finger and briefed me on the sign I was to look for. 'Central Line. Central Line. The red one. The red one,' I chanted to myself.

My mum handed me my travel card and told me to watch what she did, and then we advanced towards the barriers, my mum in front of me and my dad behind. I watched as my mum put her card in the slot, and I saw the machine suck it up and spit it out on top. She pulled it out and moved through the open gate and then turned to me. My young brain could feel the pressure of all the commuters behind me. I fumbled with my card and tried to insert it in the slot. In a flash the machine sucked it in and spat it out, so I grabbed it quickly and moved forwards. I felt a surge of adrenaline and pride. I thought, 'I'm like a real Londoner!'

I glued myself to my parents' sides to stay safe and tried to copy how they wove their way through the crowd. I read the signs ahead of time so I wouldn't slow and clog the cacophonous flood of people-traffic around me. I listened to how my parents' calmly spoke to each other: 'Oh no. That section is closed for maintenance. It looks like we'll need to figure out a different route. That happens sometimes. It'll be okay. Between us, we can find a way.'

Throughout the entire journey, I was in awe. I shook with fear on the steep escalators. I managed not to fall to my death in the gap between the train and the platform. And once inside the carriage, my parents whispered instructions to me and pointed out the little map on the side that showed the stops so I could track where I was. I watched how others braced themselves so they wouldn't fall when the carriage took off, and I saw how *not* to look people in the eyes. I learned how to snaggle a seat during a stop and when it was appropriate to give up my seat for others. In short, I learned how to navigate the complexities of the Tube.

Finally we hopped off – again, minding the gap (oh, I'm good) – and we made our way through the maze of tunnels, escalators and people, back up to the outside. When I emerged on to the street, I was a new girl. I, Rachel, had conquered the Tube! On the return trip back to our hotel, I insisted on going first in our little family travel band, so I could pretend I was alone.

Years later, on another trip to London, I begged my parents to let me go on a mini-journey by myself, and one afternoon they agreed.

By then I had gained the sheer confidence in my ability to navigate the Tube's complexities on my own, even when lines were closed. Decades later, what was once an overwhelming puzzle to figure out eventually became my mundane daily commute.

Just as experiencing the complexities of London's Underground was overwhelming to me as a child, experiencing the complexities of family life and ministry may feel overwhelming for children now. But when our children feel connected to us, we can help them engage with and navigate the complexities of church politics, hypocrisy and even conflict. These can be very confusing topics for children and teens to understand, and many situations may be beyond their immediate understanding.

We hear nightmare stories of how church leaders' children have suffered stress, and often it's in these areas of handling complex conflicts that are inherent in church leadership. Some children are exposed to church politics and conflict and are devastated by potentially unsafe adults, intense emotions and the impact it has on their parents. Others may be confused by seeing how their parent is one way at home but changes around the congregation. They may be hurt by the idea that the same people in the congregation who are 'nice' can also be aggressive, sinful and complex. Consequently, many church leaders' children, when they are in their older years, experience a disdain for hypocrisy and struggle to understand how the church can exist like that.

Church conflict and stress can create significant fear within us as church leaders, because much of it we cannot fix or change. But with the right tools, we can use our connection with our children to help them understand and engage with these complex issues without being damaged by them. Let's first explore these two tools, and then we will apply them to church conflict and hypocrisy.

If you have engaged with Parenting for Faith courses or books, you will recognise these as the first two of the five Key Tools. They are significant skills that we talk about in coaching our children to meet and know God in their daily life, but they are also crucial for us as church leaders to build and maintain connection with our children, as well as to help them navigate and understand the complexities of living in a church world.

1 Creating Windows

I live in a terraced house. I always love looking in the windows of other houses on my road to see how my neighbours arrange the inside of their homes. (Yes, my husband is horrified at me.) Our houses all have the same blueprint, but as I walk down the road, I can look through others' windows and see how number 60 added a room divider, which I love, and number 72 arranged the couches differently, which I think makes the room look smaller. As I look in the windows, I learn from all the other people's experiments and choices. Later, I reflect on my own choices and consider where I might want to make changes. I find it fascinating.

When we get to see into other people's lives, even if only by a glance through a window, we can learn a little of how they're feeling and arranging their thoughts. We can see what life with God looks like for them, and how their friendships with others impact their lives. When someone else is generous enough to create windows into their internal life with God, and into their thoughts and feelings about life and relationships, then we are encouraged to reflect on our own journeys, learn new skills and approaches, and ultimately change and grow.

When I was learning to navigate the Underground for the first time, I watched my parents to see what they did and how they reacted to what was happening around us. Did they look peaceful? When they were confused, how did they handle it? How did they walk and position themselves so they didn't get squashed? How did they feel when a section turned out to be closed for maintenance? By seeing their experience, I learned how to navigate my own.

Our children need us to create windows into our lives so they can glance in and see what a life lived with God in ministry looks like, how we emotionally and spiritually navigate our days and how we think and feel about it all. When we create these windows, we can form a deeper and more solid connection with our children, to help them understand and learn how to find their own way through complex scenarios and to enable them to grow in their faith.

But creating windows doesn't happen naturally, particularly for church leaders. Our internal life tends to be private, which means that our children can be left on the outside only seeing our actions and choices, rather than understanding our internal thoughts, feelings and interactions with God. If we can deliberately begin to create windows into our life with God and into our experience of ministry, then we can significantly help our children to feel more connected to us. And by doing this, they will better be able to see that we are the same person through all the different scenarios we encounter at work and home, in ministry and while relaxing. We can help them understand how their heart, thoughts and emotions *can* cope with ministry.

Remember, you are God's gift to your children, to walk alongside them through all that life brings their way. Your imperfect, figuring-out-how-to-walk-with-God presence in their lives is a vital part of that gift. Try making choices to deliberately let your children see the internal thoughts, feelings and options you have, as well as glimpses into how you and God are negotiating those options together. Here are a few possibilities:

- Let your children see more of your private moments. Sometimes, when we are doing our work at home, we shut the door to keep the noise and distraction out. But when we do that, our children may never see what our time with God looks like. They may never see us pray on our own, genuinely worship alone or read the Bible to feed ourselves. They may never see what it looks like to write a sermon with God. Children need to see us doing what we value, and they need to see what the connection between God and ministry really looks like. By occasionally leaving our office door opened a crack, we can create a window into our lives so our children can see and learn what spending time alone with God is all about. Jesus did this all the time. He urged his followers to pray in private, not on display for others to see (Matthew 6:5), and yet the disciples were close enough to overhear and record some of his prayers for us. They got a close-up view of what Jesus' connection with God looked like and so learned and incorporated those examples into their own lives.

- For a moment, it's okay to create a window into your feelings about your job. It's alright to be tired and say to your children, 'Sometimes my heart gets tired of doing so much, and I need to spend some time with people who understand the ups and downs of my job because they are doing it too. That's why I love going to these network meetings. They make me feel not alone, and by sharing with others and hearing other people's stories, I feel stronger when I come back!' Or you might say to your children, 'I love seeing all these people hear about Jesus over Christmas. I know it's a lot of work, and I feel sad and sometimes regretful that I can't spend as much time at home as I want to, but I'm also in awe of how God meets people. I have lots of emotions about it.'

- When you have a difficult pastoral issue before you, like a key member dying, feel free to create a window into your feelings. You might say, 'I'm heartbroken that this person is dying, and I'm so hoping that God does a miracle right now. But I'm just not seeing it. My heart is just heavy. But God says he is close to the broken-hearted. And you know what? I'm definitely feeling broken-hearted. It doesn't make my heart less sad. It just feels like I'm not alone in my sadness. God is with me.'

By creating windows into your emotions and life with God, you build connection with your children and enable them to see what your life with God is like in the middle of ministry.

2 Framing

If you have ever parented an under-five child, then you know this skill well. Life with a tiny person is all about framing. Framing is when you show children something specific and then explain to them what they're looking at. We do this non-stop with our children when they are tiny. For example, we frame activities for our children, like how to cross the road: 'This is a road crossing. See the cars zooming by? We need to wait for the green man sign. Wait for it… Look – the green man! Okay now, look both ways, because sometimes people don't see their red light and the car keeps coming. Look both ways. Good! Here we go!'

We also frame emotions for them: 'Oh no, your sister is crying! She is feeling sad because you took her toy. She wants it back. Look how sad she is feeling. Let's give the toy back. Look! She is happy again. You helped her, and it made her happy.' From explaining how the world works to describing emotions, we are constantly framing the world for our children because we want them to understand.

When my parents were helping me navigate the Tube, they deliberately took time to teach me about the London Underground and how it worked, and they also taught me those little, practical details of how to use the Tube successfully. They framed the experience for me so I could navigate it better the next time and eventually navigate it on my own.

Our children need an enormous amount of family life and ministry framed for them. If we don't frame how ministry works and how we feel in the middle of it, then our children are left on their own to try to figure it out for themselves. And that is when clergy children begin to develop some of their damaging beliefs.

Here are a few examples of framing:

- When you have a long ministry morning at church and you need some downtime, rather than saying to your children, 'I'm tired and need my space,' take a second to frame the situation for them: 'I love my job. I love loving people, teaching them about what God says and having tough conversations with them. But phew! It's like I just ran a marathon, and my brain and my heart and even my soul are exhausted. I'm going to go rest for 45 minutes and recharge, and then I'd love to come out and play with you.'

- When discussing the early morning traditional service with your child, you can explain, 'I know it looks boring to you, but to those people, they love it. Everyone is different, and everyone meets with God in different ways. You like upbeat music and lots of energy, and this group of people really likes to meet with God in the quiet. They value liturgy and hymns to help them focus on God. Just as we would like them to broaden their experience and welcome more upbeat music into church, we also need to honour how they meet with God and broaden our own experiences of meeting God in the quiet.'

These two skills, Creating Windows and Framing, become incredibly important tools for us to use to help our children see consistency and safety in the face of church conflict and apparent hypocrisy.

Church stress and conflict

Conflict makes church leadership difficult. Whether mild or full-blown, church conflict is an inevitable part of our lives. If it is a part of our lives, it could also become a part of our children's lives.

How we deal with this conflict, and how we coach our children through it, plays a significant part in helping them flourish as members of a ministry family. Martin Weber, in his PhD dissertation,[7] found that there is 'no greater cause of attrition than to attempt to shield children from knowledge of, or to resist discussion about, church or denominational conflict'. His findings showed that 'parents avoiding the topic of church conflict' was the number one issue that pushed children away from the church.

When we have a good connection with our children, we have opportunities to talk with them about everything and anything. It isn't about simply explaining issues; it's about creating windows into how we deal with conflicts and framing situations in ways they can understand and can see God in.

Now, this doesn't mean that our children become our venting team or that we report to them all the conflicts of the church. On the contrary. They should not be included in the constant swirl of information surrounding conflicts. But it *is* vital that we watch out for their knowledge of a conflict, create space to talk about the problem, explain where it is appropriate to do so and, most importantly, show them how we are dealing with it and how they can too.

There are times when your children may overhear raised voices at a meeting in your house. It might be worth asking:

> Did any of you hear some voices raised last night? How did you feel? It was a tough meeting. It happens sometimes. We were discussing the possibility of some changes, and some people found those changes difficult. Remember when we had to move, and we all had lots of emotions about it? Some of us were upset. Some didn't want the change to happen. Some felt helpless or scared, and others were excited. Some of us felt all those feelings at once! Part of my job is to help this church grow and follow what God is saying, and that means some change. Last night people were experiencing lots of emotions,

and I'm so grateful my job is to listen to them, learn from their wisdom and help them through those emotions. But it can get a bit noisy. It can be very tiring for me, and it's hard not to be offended sometimes. I had a good chat with God about it afterwards, and that brought me peace. I'm sorry if it worried you or made you scared. Do you have any questions? Let's make a plan, so if it gets noisy next time, you don't have to feel those feelings. Maybe you can turn music on? And I'll also make sure I ask them to lower their voices.

Whether it's people seeking your resignation or a small disagreement within your congregation, if your kids know something about it, they may feel stress, become confused or secretly worry about it. By keeping a good connection with them and by proactively seeking to create windows into how you are dealing with it, you establish a healthy dialogue to coach your children through church conflict.

Hypocrisy

Sometimes we get whiplash when we are trying to swap hats, particularly when it comes to needing to look kind and peaceful or ready and welcoming when we are feeling anything but. Over and over, I hear the same stories when talking with families of those in church leadership. The scenario goes something like this:

People are going to arrive for the service planning meeting at 7.30 pm. It's 7.20 and Mum is upstairs trying to wrangle the youngest two who are running around each other. The children are in no way ready for bed, because bath time was late. Mum deploys the 'serious voice' with discipline quick on its heels. Downstairs, the lounge is still cluttered with toys, a plate streaked with jam and some random pants draped on the couch. Dad is trying to tidy up while also being engaged in a tense 'conversation' with his 14-year-old. The volume is increasing with the son putting forth passionate arguments and eye rolls for why he should not have to do a certain chore again. Just then, the doorbell rings. Someone has arrived early.

Dad snaps at his son, 'I don't have time for this. Go upstairs. I have my meeting now.' Mum runs down to open the door while the kids continue to scream upstairs. Everyone is frazzled, stressed or frustrated. Mum and Dad stop and take a quick pause to summon their strength and display all smiles, and then they open the door: 'Welcome to our home!'

While this might not be your scenario this week, versions of this regularly play out across the country. Whether it's the cranky walk to church or the stressful getting out of the house, we often feel the pressure to 'put on our faces' for the congregation.

When we do this, our children can begin to feel that sometimes we hide our authentic self and put on a false self to perform for the church – to make it appear that we are better, or are doing better, than we really are. This can become problematic for our children. It comes to the fore in two scenarios:

1 *When they watch us change for others* – Children can see us go from exhausted at home to high-energy at church, or from annoyed and angry at home to happy and loving at church. Children may also see the reverse: us having loads of patience for others at church, but then snapping at them on the walk home.

2 *When they are forced to participate in the hypocrisy by sweeping away authentic home life or conflict to appear perfect* – Every family has stories like this, but it is particularly pronounced in church families. Our scenario is different because of the flow of the intrusion of the congregation *into* home life. The requirement to be a family around the congregation at church or at an event can mean that the switching back and forth between home life and work life happens frequently. When we feel the need to switch into 'church leader mode', we expect our family to switch

into 'church leader *family* mode'. And for each family, this 'mode' looks different. For some, it's putting on the face that they are one big, happy, peaceful family. For others, it's the family proactively participating in selfless serving. For still others, it's the family taking a backseat and staying out of the way. It means that we, as church leaders, expect our families – in the snap of the fingers – to drop all of their emotions and struggles and to perform for the congregation, just as we will.

Whichever scenario occurs, eventually our children will begin to struggle with it.

Church leaders aren't the only ones who have a 'work self' and a 'home self'. My father was a police officer. He behaved one way when he was on the job as a police officer in a dangerous city and another way when he was hanging out at home as my dad. That made sense, because his work and home lives did not intersect. But our situation as church leaders is very different. Our work life, home life and *church* life are all muddled together in the same location, which is a real problem. We are simultaneously trying to do our job, parent and disciple our children in their walk with God and in their own lay work with the church *all at the same time*. We have more considerations than other parents and we have to find an integrated way to wear all the hats at the same time. It can feel a bit unfair that we as church leaders must negotiate that flip from work-self to home-self differently from others, but this is where connection, creating windows and framing become very important.

When you are experiencing a lot of family stress and people begin to arrive for a meeting, it can be easy just to command, 'Upstairs! We will deal with this later,' or, 'For now, put your happy faces on, welcome people, and we will talk about this tomorrow.' Then when your children get upstairs or out of the room, they overhear you laughing and happily interacting with your guests, and they remember that just seconds or minutes before, you were angry. This is when children begin to piece together in their heads that they, and all of us, have to hide our stress and arguments from people because we're pretending to be perfect, even though we're not.

It might be worth taking some time when you aren't in a family conflict to do some framing about how to handle these types of scenarios. You might frame it by saying:

> Have you ever felt like we have to perform happiness for other church people when we don't feel happy at all? I never want you to feel like that. I know sometimes if our family has stress right before a meeting and we can't resolve the issue or finish our conversation, then you might feel as if we are trying to rush away and not let people see our normal family life. That's not what it is. For me, I always want to make sure that I have the time to listen and respond well to you all, but because other people are coming here for a meeting, I know I can't. That makes me feel sad and frustrated. I'm aware that when people come to our house, I want them also to feel welcomed and peaceful. It can be really hard to know the right thing to do. For right now it means that I ask you to go upstairs, and we plan to continue the conversation later. Then I push pause on my feelings about our discussion, and I try to find my peace because I don't want to put my stress on to others. That's why you may hear me sounding cheerful to others. But I'm not sure that's working for me or for you guys. Can you help us find a new pattern to use for when we are stressed, so our guests feel loved and welcomed, and we as a family can feel like we settle well together?

Whenever you feel like your children see a discrepancy in how you are at work and home, or in how you transition quickly between the two, take a minute or two to frame it and create windows into your experience. When you frame and create windows, you enable your children to see that you are the same authentic person in different circumstances, rather than someone who is performing for others and expecting others to perform too. You can also ask your children to create windows into their experience and frame for you how it looks from their point of view. All of this enables us to find a way forwards through connection.

Find ways to talk to the congregation authentically. It's okay to say, 'Come on in! Bedtime is running a bit late, so would you mind answering the door and welcoming the others as they come. Tea and biscuits are ready in the kitchen. Can you cover me while I get my kids in bed? You know how it goes!' Or when you arrive at church, and two of your children are crying, it's okay to say to others, 'Tough morning. I'm sure you've had many, so you understand!' This invites people to understand, while not being put upon, and creates space for you to acknowledge that your family needs you without giving away too much information.

In whatever situation you and your family find yourselves in, if your connection with your children is strong, then you can create opportunities to help them through it. If you create windows into how you feel and think, and frame for your children what they are looking at, then you will be able to coach them through the myriad of church complexities that will come their way.

You *can* help your children flourish in conflict and expectation. What a blessing we have to lay a foundation for them in how to find God, peace and joy in the midst of leadership, ministry and family.

II

Prioritised

4

The power of feeling prioritised

One of the most potent images in scripture is that of God as our parent (and us as God's children). There is something special in that analogy that we innately understand. Our Father has chosen us. He has sacrificed for us. He has sought us out, rescued us from sin and given us a hope of eternal life with him. Because of what God has done and continues to do, we know that he, our ultimate parent, sees us as precious, valued and wanted children. We do not deserve the love and attention that God pours upon us, and when we experience his love, we feel an overwhelming sense of our worth in him.

We see this echoed in our human relationships. There is something fantastic about being someone's child. Among the billions of people in our world today, each of us, as a child, belongs to only a few of them. We have a unique relationship with our parents, one that isn't dependent on performance or neediness. This relationship is exclusive and comes with unique privileges, access and undeserved favour purely because of who we are: their child.

Within our own families, when these parent-child relationships are functioning well, then our children experience a deep sense of peace and safety, whether they are toddlers, teens or adults. They sense they are safe, loved, valued and are of the utmost priority to us, and we need to preserve that. Our children need to rest in knowing that even though we are church leaders, we will still give them priority in our considerations, our time, our attention and our heart.

When our children feel they are a priority in our lives, then they will not see members of the congregation as competitors vying for our attention, nor the church as an organisation that is attempting to steal us away from them. They can:

- value the church and the congregation
- feel peacefully secure in our affection, care and attention, and be comfortable with seeing us give our time and attention to the church
- develop a healthy understanding of the role of a church leader and what it is like to serve people passionately without sacrificing family or relationships.

Being a better juggler

One of the stresses of church-leader families is the juggling act of life. How do we balance the different needs of our congregation and our family? Both want our time. Both need our attention. It can feel like there is constant pressure not to take away too much from either side.

If we sense that our children are feeling disconnected from us or are resenting our congregation or leadership obligations, then we might think the answer lies in simply establishing better boundaries. We tell ourselves, 'I just need to get better at swapping hats.' Sometimes we can blame our schedule and think, 'I just need to carve out more time to spend at home.'

Prioritisation goes much deeper than just establishing boundaries and carving out space. It isn't necessarily about *what* you say yes and no to; it's about *how* we make those choices and communicate to our family about them.

Within this section, we are going to look at how to structure ministry life in a way that helps our children feel they are a priority to us. This doesn't mean that they always need to be the first consideration in every decision we make. It does mean, though, that in whatever we choose to do, our children should feel that their needs, their place in our life and their relationship with us *are* of constant value to us and that we make choices to protect that.

In the next chapter, we will look at how to negotiate the dynamic of children feeling as if their needs are in competition with the congregation's, thereby positioning us in the middle. In chapter 6, we will look at how to ensure that our time with our children makes them feel they're a priority in our life, rather than an unacknowledged person in the room. And in chapter 7, we will be putting all this together and looking at the tricky situation of working from home and hosting events in the home, and how our children can still feel like a priority even in that muddled space.

5

Removing the competition of needs

There is one phrase in traditional wedding vows that I find especially powerful: 'forsaking all others'. It's a phrase that says, 'I choose you, and I'll say no to everyone else.' It says, 'I will proactively defend your place in my life.' It says, 'You can be safe and secure in your absolute importance to me.' This vow is a declaration that whatever comes, whoever we meet in the future, wherever our choices take us in the whole world, I will preserve and protect 'us'. It is a bold and mighty vow. It brings to the relationship the safety, security and freedom needed to grow.

Although we may never say this phrase to our children in a ceremony, our children grow to trust in that same sense of priority. There is an exclusivity to our relationship with them that says, 'You are my children, no others. You have special access to me, the security of my love and affection, and my commitment to put you before others.' This kind of relationship enables our children to feel safe, secure and free to grow, because they know that we are going to fight to keep them as a priority in our lives.

Our kids are rarely worried that other children at school or in the community will wander in and take their place in our heart. They know they are important to us and a priority in our world, by the sheer fact that they *are* our children. But if we could step into our children's hearts for a moment, we might find a niggling worry invading their sense of being a priority – a worry that we may not be able or willing to prioritise family over church because the need of the church is so large. They can begin to feel as if they are in a competition – a competition of needs.

Our children see glimpses of the enormous job we do. They see the constant needs of the church and its people, and they see its impact on us as we juggle leadership. They are proud of us and want to help us, and they love us a lot. If we aren't careful, however, some of them learn a new kind of maths – the church's needs are greater, therefore their needs are lesser.

Sometimes our children begin to think that what dictates their parents' decisions is who has the greatest need. Their desire to play with their dad versus a person in hospital who is dying of cancer and needs their pastor: church wins. Their desire to have their mum read to them at bedtime versus the vicar being needed for the church annual gathering: church wins. Their need to talk to their parent about a tough day at school versus a flood at the church hall: church wins. The sheer numbers are against our children if they begin to feel as if they're in a one-to-one competition with the church and its people. They'll never be able to compete with the greater demands of congregation, volunteers, buildings and denomination.

This feeling in children of losing the competition of needs is formed slowly and subtly, which is the problem. No parent announces, 'Children, I am now a church leader, and every single congregant is now more important than you. My work is also more important than you. You have been notified.' But over time, our children can begin to feel that this is true. As that happens, worry slowly sneaks into their hearts and minds, and sometimes they can't even articulate what they're beginning to feel. As church leaders, it's important that we proactively address and dispel these feelings, because our children need to know that there is no competition. They need to be secure in our commitment to them before all others.

In the rest of this chapter, we will look at ways, via our language and our choices, to reinforce to our children the understanding that their relationship with us will always be preserved and protected.

Our language matters

In chapter 3 we talked about framing: explaining a topic or experience to our child so that they better understand it. In the normal course of everyday life, our casual conversations with our children can end up unintentionally framing a situation in ways we don't anticipate. If we want our children to feel that they are a priority to us, then when we we need to be aware of how important our language can be.

Naturally, as parents and church leaders we tend to be open with our families about where we are and what we are doing. We like to tell our children or spouse what is going on in our lives and, if our schedule changes, why. When our family tries to add something to a day when we are already busy, it's easy to say, 'No, sorry. I have a work thing.' Normally these conversations are great ways of staying connected and enabling our children and spouse to hear about our day and how we feel about it. But there are times when it may be prudent to change the way we talk about a topic – change the way we frame it – in order for our children to understand what we really want them to know. When we do this, we especially need to pay attention to how we justify ourselves when we can't be there for them, particularly if we have to prioritise a church need over a family commitment or opportunity.

Our casual openness can unintentionally create a family-versus-congregation competition within our children. When we say, 'I'm going to be home late today. I just got a call that there's a lady in hospital who's very ill and it's important that I go visit her before I come home,' our children can hear, 'Helping sick people is more important than playing with you.' When we say, 'I won't be able to make it to the second performance of your choir recital. There's a funeral that needs to happen that week, and that's the only time it will work for everybody,' our children can hear, 'I decided that being at your performance wasn't important enough to pick a different time for the funeral.' Over and over our children hear that the congregation is the reason that we are unavailable to them.

Often we answer like this to demonstrate to our families that we aren't just willy-nilly avoiding them; we are unavailable because it's something important. But by framing the situation in this way, we are accidentally saying, 'See this? This is more important than you.' Our explanations can feed into a pattern of comparison and set up our children for the competition of greater and lesser needs.

The answer isn't to suddenly change our schedules so that we are 100% available to our families or to prioritise our family's requests to the extreme. We have a job, and we are called to do it well. That means we can't be everywhere at once, and we must make hard decisions. Sometimes we can't be home on time or be at every performance. That's just life. But what we *can* do is frame the situation in a way that strengthens our connection and affirms to them that their priority in our life is still strong.

All we need to do is change the focus from 'this is the good reason why I chose them over you' to simply 'I really want to be there, but I've got a job thing and so I can't. I'm disappointed I can't be there, but here's how we can find another time and space to experience connection, so we don't miss out on too much.'

In the example of needing to swing by the hospital to do a pastoral visit, you can say:

> I've got something to do before I come home, and I'm not sure how long I'll be. I'm sorry. I know you are waiting, and I appreciate your patience. Can you set up the game so when I get home we can get to playing straight away?

In the example of needing to put a funeral on the same day as your child's second performance, you could say:

> I'm so sorry, but a work thing came up, and so I can't make the second performance. I'm gutted. I hate saying I can be there and then letting you down. Can we make sure that we film it so you can show it to me later that night? Or maybe I can FaceTime to see that hard bit of the song you've been practising?

By speaking this way, you are framing for your child that you recognise the change and you acknowledge the disappointment for both of you. Furthermore, you can affirm the many ways you are interested in your child's activity and demonstrate how you are proactively trying to ensure that both of you can make the best of a less-than-ideal situation.

If your children ask what the work situation is, you can either tell them or not. It's not a secret, but neither is it relevant to the honest apology, appreciation and relationship connection that you are focused on. This approach also preserves your ability to share your stories later, as sharing about your work life is an important part of connection. So later, when you're playing or eating dinner, you can debrief your week and create windows into your life by saying:

> I needed this laugh. There is one woman from the church who is quite ill with cancer, and I've been visiting her in hospital to encourage her and pray for her. We have been praying for ages, but she is still ill, and it doesn't look good. I love being able to be with her, but this journey is heartbreaking. You guys help me so much. Just being with you makes me feel so joyful. Thanks for being my family.

Communicate the 'Yes'

Children and teens in a ministry context can easily feel like the world is full of 'No's:

- 'No, you can't run around at church.'
- 'No, you can't kiss my face while I try to lead a service.'
- 'No, I can't do bedtime reading because I have a meeting.'
- 'No, we can't go visit our relatives for the long weekend because I have to work on Sunday.'

It can make our children feel as if life is ruled by the church.

An easy and simple fix is to help your children know their options for 'Yes'. For example:

- 'You may not run in church, *but feel free* to lie on the floor under the pew, or stand on the chair next to me, or hold my hand, or even lean on me, as long as you stay within arm's length of me.'
- 'You may not kiss my face while I lead worship, *but may I have* a hug and kiss before I go up to preach?'
- 'I cannot do bedtime reading tonight, *but can you help me problem-solve* how we can do some reading at another time?'

Children and teens may find it hard to creatively problem-solve for options, especially when the parameters are unclear. The more you work with them to discover their options for 'Yes', the more they will learn to see the constant opportunities, rather than settle for a wall of 'No'.

When we choose *how* we talk about a situation, we can break down any perceived competition our children feel between themselves and the church or congregation. We then gain the freedom to discuss with them our job and the inherent joys and difficulties that come with it from a perspective of relationship rather than from one that sets up a competition.

Our choices matter

As we frame for our children how our relationship with them is a priority for us, we should back up what we say with action. Our children look to see the truth of our words in our choices and actions. How we choose to act speaks volumes when it comes to our children becoming confident and feeling safe in the exclusive place of priority that they have in our lives.

Choose to be a parent

It can be so easy to fall into the pattern of simply managing our children rather than parenting them, especially when we are with our congregations. We know that as leaders, we need to bring attention, care and responsibility to our job, and so we can be tempted to put our parenting on pause until later, when we have space to actively parent again. This delay in parenting can create a sort of performance pressure: 'When we go out, son, I expect you to behave and be perfect and leave me alone. If that doesn't happen, then when we get home, there will be consequences!'

If we are going to parent our children while we are with our congregations, then it's helpful to first think about what our children expect from us as parents. Our children expect us to:

- respond to their presence
- express affection, care and compassion towards them
- take care of their practical needs
- answer their questions
- discipline them
- make opportunities for them to connect to us, God and church.

While we can't always fulfil each of these expectations to the extent that we want to, we can still do some of this. We need to be kind to ourselves and to our families and permit ourselves to parent in the same private, safe way that we would if we weren't church leaders.

Once I was preaching, and during the sermon I noticed that my seven-year-old son had walked up to the front and was standing at the base of the platform, watching me. He wasn't disruptive; he was just standing there. I frantically looked around for my husband, who was nowhere to be found. I kept preaching. I gave the crazy eyes to my friend that clearly communicated, 'What in the world is my kid doing? Please can you get him? He clearly has no idea where his dad is. His default is just to stand next to the parent he knows, and that happens to be me right now.' My friend laughed at the joke I was telling in the sermon. Evidently my crazy eyes weren't communicating what I had hoped.

My kid needed me to parent, and I was busy preaching. Eventually, I thought, 'All my kid needs is his mum to tell him what to do. He's a bit lost.' So I made up a talk-to-your-neighbour question and said to the crowd, 'Have you ever felt like nothing would ever be right again, like Joseph? Turn to the person next to you and share that time in your life.' And then I knelt on the platform, hugged my kid and said, 'Are you okay? It looks like you don't know where to sit.' He nodded and said, 'I can't find Daddy.' I glanced around and found a familiar face. 'Look, there's Kate. Why don't you go sit with her?' I waved and caught Kate's eye and pointed to my kid. She nodded and waved him over. I watched my son's shoulders relax, and then he wrapped his arms around my neck, and I kissed his head. He went over to Kate and happily sat with her for the rest of the service. Sometimes you just have to parent.

Over and over, I hear stories of church leaders who chose to be parents in the midst of ministry, and I hear how their choices signi-ficantly impacted their children's feelings about the church. Here are some examples.

- One child of a church leader told me that when he had an illness and was in a lot of pain and stress, his parents would take turns staying home with him. He remembers those sick days as precious times because of the comfort and care he received from his parents. Even as church leaders, sometimes we need to choose to be the one who takes a day off to stay home with a sick child, or the one who works from home with a bundle of feverish hotness against our arm and the original *Star Wars* trilogy playing on TV. Children remember our presence with them and the care we give them in those times when we choose them over work.

- Another church leader told me the story of when she didn't go on her own church's weekend away because she promised her son she would take him to an open day at his third-choice university. Because both events had been scheduled for the same weekend, she had to make a choice, and she chose her child. The church staff and congregation kept sending her and her son pictures with 'we miss you' love notes and good wishes for the open day. The son was overwhelmed with how encouraging and supportive the church was to both of them.

- Once I was working at a church, and we were in the middle of the worship when the leader who was scheduled to preach received a text from his wife. She had texted that their daughter had fallen and cut her head; it was bleeding a lot, but she wasn't showing any signs of concussion. His wife wrote that she was heading to the hospital with the other kids so there was no need for him to come immediately; after church would be fine. He leaned over and whispered the news to me, and I could tell he was concerned, especially as this child didn't do well with pain and blood and she was attached to her dad when she was in need. After a brief argument with me in the front row, I took his sermon notes and sent him to the hospital. The daughter was overwhelmed. Many, many years later, this now-teenager still tells that story of the time when her dad left the church to hold her and made her laugh while she got a butterfly bandage. That one incident convinced her that her father prioritised her over the church, and as a result she became much more generous when he needed to be gone from home because she knew that when it came down to it, she would be chosen.

I've heard stories of people having to leave evening budget meetings to run upstairs and calm down a child who just soiled himself, and I've seen a bishop stoop down to tie his grandchild's shoe. We all share a deep and powerful desire to serve the church well, to sacrifice and give our lives for the calling to lead these churches. I understand and value the importance of giving our best to our congregations. I also understand the arguments of those who feel that church leaders are distracted by their families when they allow themselves to be parents, but I respectfully disagree with those arguments. I feel that when we let ourselves be parents in the midst of our ministries, we call our congregations to do the same.

After situations when I obviously had to take a moment to privately parent, I have had parents come up to me, some in tears, thanking me for doing so – for showing them we are all in the same boat, and for making them feel it's okay to parent in church. Our people want to be integrated people, and they too struggle with swapping hats.

I want my kids' team volunteers to feel comfortable and confident in being a leader and a parent. I want my single-parent home group leaders to feel confident in hosting groups in their homes, knowing that they might need to disappear halfway through meetings to kiss and pray over their kids at bedtime.

We *can* create a culture where integration is possible, and it starts with our leadership teams. It starts with us valuing each other, supporting and helping each other to prioritise our families, and covering for each other when needed. It takes us being open with our congregations and letting them know that we will still be parenting as we lead. Let's be known as people who are *for* each other's family life. Let's be known as a community which says, 'Invest in your family! We release you and we have your back.' Let's create a culture where our churches are known for having flourishing family lives. But first, let it start with us. Let's give ourselves the freedom to be integrated people, leading our congregations and parenting our children well – together.

6

Tuning in

Can you remember one of your best days of holiday time with your family? Maybe it was a day kayaking on a lake or your child's first experience at the beach. Maybe it was the time all of you hiked across the moor, singing songs and spotting animals. Can you remember what it felt like? That sense of being free from stress and fully present to the joys and delights of time with family?

Holidays can be so precious because they offer us and our children those times of togetherness, of feeling that what is happening within our family, right at that moment, is the most important thing of all. When we are in those moments, we become fully available and attentive to what is happening, and we enjoy the time together. Sometimes it takes a while for us to achieve a level of rest that enables us to feel present. Church leaders' children repeatedly talk about the good memories of holidays with their parents and how rare that sense of family can be in the swirl of ministry life.

I believe that it is possible to give everyone, including church leaders and their families, that same sense of peace, joy and present-ness *within* our everyday lives, so our families aren't just surviving through a time of disconnection until the next day off or the next holiday. One of the significant findings that has come out of the research interviews has been that, while most children would like more time with their parents, it is the parents' *availability and attention* that enable that time to be significant for children. When we figure out how to enable our children to feel that strong sense of belonging, they can feel that they are a priority in our lives. Even when most of our day is not spent with them, if we can manage to ensure that the time we *do* spend with them is excellent, connecting time, then their sense of being valued is strengthened. When our children feel they are a priority in our lives, their fears, worries, stress and sense of competition can drop, and they can enjoy us and the church with more open arms.

How can we make our children feel prioritised through our availability and attention? The adjustments may be smaller than you think.

Making our availability count

One of the joys of working for a church is that our schedules are often flexible. We can make time to attend the third performance of the oboe quartet or do the school run. Flexibility can give us more time to be home with the kids in the afternoon or go on school trips with them. It can be a wonderful thing.

The flip side of that coin is that our jobs are changeable. Some weeks we have meetings; some weeks we don't. Some days we can be home at 4.00 pm; others we can only come home after an evening meeting. Some days we can take our child to their swimming lesson; others we can't.

Church leaders' children can sometimes struggle with this lack of routine, and the stress of it all can sap the grace from them. Many of them describe the feeling that the church or God has 'stolen' their parent. They get a sense that at any moment they will discover that the parent whom they thought was going to be home is now gone, as if the church had snapped them away for some unknown need, emergency or meeting. For our children, this inconsistency can feel chaotic and makes them unsure about when they can count on you. The unpredictability in a parent's schedule can make teens, in particular, feel unimportant. Teens can often store things up to talk about, and then they discover that the moment they had planned to talk with you, you've become mysteriously unavailable.

What is surprising, though, is that our children's sense of church intrusion is often not rooted in reality. Typically, a church leader's schedule is set weeks in advance, but to our children it feels unpredictable – it seems there is always a crisis or an unexpected situation that pulls us away. They don't see our long-range schedule that changes week to week.

Here are a few ways to reduce this stress of unpredictability for our children and help them feel safe, peaceful and that they are our priority.

1 Make a calendar

Have a calendar or schedule where everyone can see it and be reminded of it. With children who have phones, you can sync calendars or use a family calendar app that everyone has access to. Many families have found it useful to also have a calendar on the fridge or on a wall in the house. Once a week use the calendar to talk about your upcoming schedule, so that everyone can see where you will be and when, and how their schedules tie in with yours. That way everyone can be on the same page of who will be where. Any extraordinary circumstance that arises because of the church can be seen for what it is: an aberration and extraordinary situation, rather than one more day that the church interrupts home life.

Meeting together to briefly talk through the weekly schedule can also be a time for you to create windows into your choices, when you can highlight how this week is busier than you wanted and you can apologise, or when you can display how open your schedule is and plug in lots of extra protected family time in the gaps. You also then have the opportunity to problem-solve what to do as a family if the schedule looks particularly tight or if you need to work as a team to organise lifts, movements and connection time. When you do this, your children can see how much family time actually exists, how it is protected and how your schedule is merely a work schedule. They can feel that family is a priority to you because all of you are figuring it out together as a unit.

2 Be faithful

Faithfulness is central to our children's sense that they're a priority to us, knowing that their parents care enough to keep their word. If you say you are going to be home at 5.00 pm, be home at 5.00 pm. If you say you will do bedtime, do bedtime. Every time we speak, our children take it as a promise. We can get so used to working with a flexible schedule that we forget that faithfulness is crucial to our children. You would be surprised at what little things children consider to be important.

One church leader told me that her daughter would be unreasonably angry with her when occasionally, at the last minute, she couldn't pick her up from school. Sometimes it would be because she would get tied up in a budget meeting or because a pastoral meeting went on for too long. Whenever it happened, she would call a friend who had a child at the same school and ask her to pick up her daughter as well, and then she would meet them at her friend's house later. After attending one of Parenting for Faith's Parenting as Church Leaders Days,[8] she discussed this pattern of pick-ups with her child and found that, although it was only a four-minute walk home, her child considered that to be their very important connection time together. Every day this daughter looked forward to spending these special four minutes walking home with her mum. In the parent's view, she was making sure her kid got picked up from school and it didn't matter how. To the child, this was four minutes that she could count on being with her parent every day. So when her parent didn't show up because the church needed her, she felt shoved off and abandoned.

It takes self-discipline for us to leave a meeting to ensure we get home at the promised time. Prioritising the little things in our family life is a choice, and it is an important one. Often when we are not available as planned, children don't blame the parent; they blame the church, the ministry and sometimes God.

Of course, mistakes will happen, and that is okay. When they do, we can make sure that we apologise for our mistakes in calculating when we should leave work, rather than justifying ourselves by pointing to the significance of our call, our meeting or our sermon.

To do this well, we need a team around us that supports us in this choice – a team that says, 'It's 2.45. Go, go, go! You are on school pick-up today,' or, 'No, you won't be available to lead that assembly, because you've already promised your teenager that you would buy those tickets as soon as they go live at 12 noon.' We need to build a culture among our leadership teams that faithfulness is a deep value within our jobs and within our family, and we will strive to be faithful to both.

3 Keep work time and home time separate

Doing both family and work at the same time makes children feel unimportant and undervalued. As church leaders who are also trying to parent, there is a natural tendency to try to intersperse work within our time at home, and it ends up with us not being very attentive or available to our families. Our families want more than just our bodies in the room. They want us – all of us.

Are any of these scenarios familiar to you?

- Going home to play with your children while keeping the phone close at hand so you can 'be available' in case someone calls.
- Having to take a call in the middle of a game or outing.

- Watching a movie with your children while also periodically emailing on your phone.
- Dashing away to answer a few emails when your children are playing among themselves.

We can miss that our dual-purpose efforts may be stressful for our children. It can make them feel like they are less important than our jobs. It screams out to them, 'I'm only here until something more important comes along.'

Overwhelmingly, church leaders' children have told us that they would much rather have parents stay an extra half-hour at work, and then be fully present at home when they are there, than have more time with their parents who are trying to do work at the same time as being with them.

Making our attention count

One of the many aspects of a church leader's life is that work and home get muddled together. Surgeons go to work, rummage around in people's bodies, wash up and then come home. They don't have patients showing up unexpectedly and perhaps staying in their house; they don't have surgery meetings happening four nights a week in their only lounge at home or consultations every 20 minutes on the phone through their days off. Our work life and personal life weave together in time and location, making it incredibly difficult for us to have a clear head. We are rarely far away from the next thing we need to do. While we are home, our thoughts of the day's meetings, the tasks still waiting to be done and other theological and leadership ideas keep bouncing around inside our heads. It can be so hard for us to feel fully present when we are home.

We can make a significant difference in giving our children our full attention by creating new patterns to help us adjust our *internal* lives. A holiday is so restorative because we can finally set things aside and be present with our family. What if we found a way to truly laugh with our families, and to delight in and get lost in playing with our children and enjoying our families in the tapestry of everyday life? Here are a few suggestions to help us readjust our internal lives.

Use a bridging activity

In her report on the family life of Australian clergy, psychologist and church leader Rachel Stevens, together with her husband, recommends that church leaders create a bridging behaviour, a way of transitioning, that enables their hearts and minds to move from the workspace into home space.[9] She suggests going for a run for 30 minutes, but each of us can create our own ways of transitioning from work life to home life. I know some church leaders who have a song they play in their headphones on the way home. Others make it a habit to swing by a local shop every day to get some house admin chore done, like picking up a gift for their kid's friend's birthday or paying a bill. Others call their partner or a friend for a quick chat on the way home so they can debrief their day quickly before they come through the door. Another one I know listens to a podcast as he tidies his office and puts his coat on for his walk home. Another parent I know hunts down each child when she enters the house and asks, 'What are the two most important things I need to know about your day?'

Experiment to find a bridging activity that works best for you, and then implement it to help you put down your active thoughts about your work. If you have a lot of overlap of work and home time, make your transition something small but meaningful to you. I know some church leaders who work from home and have work slippers and home slippers. Others completely swap clothes when they are off duty, literally taking off and putting on their work focus.

Open loops

Working in church leadership means having to keep track of many details at the same time: the budget, meetings, pastoral issues, problems with volunteers and so on. One way to refer to these active pieces of information in our minds is 'open loops'.[10] Until our brain can tick something off the list, it tries to keep the information active. We may find it difficult, therefore, to be fully present in the moment with our children because our brain is occupied with these open loops.

One of the keys to freeing ourselves to be present is to figure out ways to close those loops, such as by writing down the information so our brain can let go of the need to remember it. Some church leaders, for example, have a weekly calendar on their desk and, before they leave the office, jot down on it everything that is on their mind, so their brain knows that it is safely written somewhere and can close that loop. Some people send emails to themselves of things they need to get done, information they are waiting for or thoughts they want to explore further. Others use phone apps or resort to the age-old tradition of writing on Post-it notes.

Whatever you do, if you are finding yourself struggling to have a clear mind when you are at home, try out ways to close those loops rather than just telling yourself to 'be present'. Your brain may need help.

Reduce the distraction

Distraction can be one of the biggest hurdles for us in making our children feel valued. When we are in a swimming pool with our children, there is nothing to distract us from being fully present with them. But when we are home during our afternoon break, our brain and our environment can be full of distractions that pull us away from fully engaging with our children.

Manoush Zomorodi, in her book *Bored and Brilliant*, points to research which found that people who frequently switched their attention had much higher stress levels.[11] She also discovered that this kind of interruption wasn't always externally based. Most people interrupted their own thought processes and would switch to something else as often as or more often than when they were interrupted by others.

You know the scenario. You are playing with your child, and your eyes fall on your notebook with that little slip of paper dangling out the edge. Your brain says, 'Don't forget to bring that dish back to Marjorie tonight at the meeting.' Or you are in the middle of helping your child with homework, and you glance down to check your email and then think of a great example for your sermon. The more attention-switching our brain does, the more stressed we are and the less we can stay focused on the task at hand, which, in this case, is being peaceful and present with our children.

The research also showed that when we are distracted or respond to one of those many phone beeps, it takes us on average 23 minutes and 15 seconds to return to our original focus. Given the time we have with our children, if we want them to feel truly prioritised, then we need to problem-solve how to reduce the number of our own internal distractions.

Zomorodi also cites another fascinating research study focused on the power of having a phone present in a room during a conversation. Researchers at Virginia Tech analysed the quality of people's conversations without a phone present and then compared it to the conversations when a phone was present. After adjusting for all other factors, it seems that when a phone is present there is a marked drop in the quality of people's conversations. Two strangers talking without a phone in sight will have a better conversation than two family members who have a phone on the table. This study shows that simply seeing the possibility of an interruption, knowing that at any second we could lose the special position we have with our talking partner, reduces the quality of our conversation.

For those of us who blend our work and home lives together, these research findings have large implications for our connections with our children. If we want to enable our families to feel that they are a priority to us, then we need to remove the constant reminder that at any moment we may be distracted or needed by someone else who isn't present. So leave your phone out of sight. Let your kids see it's out of the room. Let your brain see it's off and out of the room. Feel free to check it when you need to, but by removing it from your physical space, you bring a lot more depth to your availability and attention towards your children. Likewise, if having your bag in the room reminds you of your next appointment or activity, move it to your home office or put it in a closet. Be aware of what is interrupting your focus and remove it.

While I was studying this, I decided to try moving my phone, as well as removing almost all the rings and buzzes from it. The result has been absolutely life-changing for me and for my ability to be present. I notice that I am so much more relaxed when I'm not constantly being reminded that there is a whole batch of people who want me, and my family has begun to believe that I'm not distracted in their presence as well.

Our children delight in being with us. If we want them to be able to enjoy us as parents and to relax at home with us, then we should ensure that we gift them with our availability and our full attention. Our time with our children is significant, powerful and important, and we can use it to help our children feel prioritised and know that we choose to be fully present with them as we connect together as family.

7

Tricky bits: working from home

Church leadership is full of unique and trying situations, but one of the toughest situations may be when we work at home. Trying to write a sermon or prepare the budget for a church AGM is difficult enough on its own; it is even more so when we have children running in and out of our office or asking to be near or giving us intense attitudes because they are having a bad day.

Working from home can be difficult for everyone involved. We church leaders can find it hard to have uninterrupted time to work, and it can take an enormous amount of focus to work through squeals, shrieks of laughter, chaos and the sense of missing out on the home life happening just outside the door. Our spouses can find it stressful to continually defend us and our work time as they're going about their own busy day. And our children can struggle to understand that their parent is home but unavailable; at times they can feel that church can reach even into their homes, reminding them that it always takes priority. Even if we have children who are in school and so only knocking around home during the holidays, if we must work from home, at some point we will have to make it work for everyone.

This situation is not new. For centuries, church leaders have struggled to negotiate home and workspace. In the 19th century, Catherine Booth and her husband William, founders of The Salvation Army, ran into the same challenges. Catherine was a prolific preacher and life at home with multiple young children was, needless to say, hard. Once she wrote to her mother about the difficulty of preparing for speaking engagements from home: 'I find the preparation is the greatest difficulty. I am subject to such constant interruptions and noise that I am often bewildered.'[12] Over time the Booths came up with their own practical solutions to meet their needs. They had eight children in their home, so one of their priorities was to soundproof Catherine's office. As the family's home was being renovated, they installed a double ceiling in her office, which was then packed with sawdust to dampen the enthusiasm of their children's noise from the playroom above. Every little bit helps.

Housing has come a long way since the mid-19th century, but the need for a secure, quiet workspace remains the same. While we may not convince our churches to install extra soundproofing in our homes, there are some things we can do to get our work done and to ensure our children continue to feel connected to us and prioritised in our lives.

Working from home has wonderful benefits. It can help us to build and grow connection with our children. It gives us the flexibility to weave in family life throughout our day. It can enable us to be available for key parts of our children's day, like at lunch or after school. It gives us a more relaxed space in which to work and think, and a more private place not to be interrupted by the congregation or staff. Working from home can be positive for all of us if we first discover life patterns that will work for everyone. Here are a few factors to consider as you try and find your own successful patterns for working at home.

Separate work time from non-work time

When we are unclear about when we work, it can create uncertainty for the children. It can feel as if we are making a series of random decisions. My kid wants me to play with play dough? No, thanks, I'd rather work. My child wants me to play with Lego? I'm in. Our decisions can seem arbitrary to our children, so they can feel as if they're competing in a tug of war, pulling for our attention and time against our commitment to our work. Creating a schedule can be a kind and gentle way of providing structure and safety for them. Feel free to say, 'I'm not free at these times, but at these times, I am free and I'll be there 100%!'

Create a clear structure for connection and transparent progress

Working from home during the day can be difficult for children who are home with us, particularly for under 5s. They know we are right there, but they aren't allowed to get to us. But they manage to, somehow. It can be exhausting and heartbreaking to push them away, so the dance becomes, 'How can I either get out of the house or get my children out of the house?' One helpful solution is to be transparent about our progress and create a clear structure for connection. If we are going to make sure our children know where their 'Yes' is, they often need to see a time scale that shows it.

I know one leader who mounted a timer on the door of his home office and whenever he went to his office to work, he set it to count down to the next 'connection time' with his children. Sometimes the kids would just watch the clock. If they were busy playing and asked their mum when Dad could join them, she would respond, 'Go look at the countdown clock.' Often the children could be heard yelling, '10, 9, 8, 7, 6, 5, 4, 3, 2, 1!', then they would burst through his office door at which point they would all cheer. The church leader then set another timer for 15 minutes of playtime. When the timer signalled playtime was over, the children would all groan and he would go back into the office and reset the work timer again.

The important factor for this technique to work is our faithfulness to ensure that no matter what is happening – whether we are in the middle of writing an email, on the phone with the bishop, deep in Hebraic analysis or making a theological breakthrough that will alter the entire future of humanity – when that alarm goes off, we *are* committed to 100% availability, focus and joy.

Another church leader felt hesitant about a timer, so she put a tick list on a whiteboard outside her office, with a list of all the things she had to do before she was free for connection time. When she finished an item from the list, she would open the door and tick it off, and her children would shout and encourage her, 'Yes! Keep going. Only two more things and you can play.'

However you choose to do it, when you create for your children a faithful, transparent, predictable way for them to have connection with you, and for you to preserve all the alone time you need, then everyone wins. Your children will feel they are an important priority to you and will know you love spending time connecting with them during the day.

When our children understand their importance to us, it sometimes creates situations when they aren't available to connect with us. One church leader loves hearing her nine-year-old say, 'I'm so sorry, but I won't be free for connection time after school today because I'm going to art club. I'll leave you a note to help you feel connected so you can focus.'

Create a transition habit

In chapter 6 we talked about creating patterns for transitioning from work life to home life so that we can be more present with our children when we come home. This principle can also work in the opposite direction to help our families understand when we are transitioning to work. Try creating a transition pattern to use in those moments when you are going to work, even when that workspace is only upstairs. Whether it's putting on office slippers or going around to all of your children to give them a 'I'm going to work now' kiss, figure out a habit that communicates to you and your children that 'work' for you is on.

Use your flexibility power

We can often feel the need to work at specific hours and times, but the power of working from home is that we can be flexible around the needs and opportunities of family. Whether we have small people at home or we're just trying to sort out holiday time, it's important to remember that we need to establish a work pattern that fits everyone. For those who have a spouse at home or another form of support, why not consider giving that person a regular morning off and taking the kids yourself? Or during school holidays why not consider splitting your workday schedule, so you do more work in the evenings and have the afternoon off with family from lunch to dinner every day?

Decide on your permeability

Church leaders have a wide range of values and standards for how comfortable they feel with being interrupted while they work. Some say they always want their children to be able to come in and interrupt because they don't want them ever to feel shut out of their lives for the sake of the church. Others say that it works best for them if they leave the door open a crack when they're available for a hug or a question, and they close the door when they're not. Others prefer the structure of 'Unless the house is on fire, please don't talk to me when I'm working'. When we decide what works best for us, it's helpful to figure out a way to communicate that to our children. Many of us bounce back and forth between a range of thoughts on this topic, so that one day we are fine with our children coming in and other days we get frustrated and tell them off. Consistency is helpful for children in this arena.

I know one church leader who had a basket of quiet toys in his office. He communicated his 'interruption' rule to his child in this way:

> Always feel free to come in for a quick hug or connection, unless I'm on the phone. If you want to be near me for a little longer when I'm working, I would love that. Here's what you can do. On the shelf is a basket of quiet toys, colouring books and headphones for listening to an audiobook. Feel free to come in and work on your own quiet project near me on the rug. That way we can both be working on our own quiet projects together, in the same room and at the same time.

There is no single right way to do this. But when we are clear on the structure, clear about our permission and clear in showing our children where their 'Yes' is, then our children can understand that our day is about a schedule rather than about a series of value judgements as to who or what is most important at the moment. Our children can feel prioritised, not because they get all of our time but because we insist on ensuring that the times of connecting with them are predictable and solid.

III

Covered

8

The gift of covering

When we enter ministry, we place our family in a unique position within a church community. For each of us, this position can feel different. Some church leaders describe the feeling as like being placed on a precarious pedestal, while others say they feel like beloved zoo animals or fish in a goldfish bowl. However you describe it, there can be a sense of being exposed and under observation, of feeling the weight of affection and expectation from a waiting crowd of congregants.

This position can create an enormous amount of blessing and opportunity for our children. They are naturally the recipients of the affection of older congregants. People in the congregation may be predisposed towards blessing them with gifts or additional treats as children of their leader. They have greater access to the physical site of the church and can become comfortable with a wide range of people from diverse abilities, backgrounds and socioeconomic areas.

This position also comes with pitfalls. It can be difficult for our children to try to grow up while being observed by a large number of people who are invested in them and who have a relationship with their parents. For our children to thrive, they need to feel not only connected and prioritised; they also need to feel *covered*.

'Covered' means that we shield them from the harsh exposure that our church leadership can subject them to, so that they are free to enjoy the benefits of the unique position their family occupies. When our children feel covered, we enable them to:

- build healthy relationships within the church on their own terms
- be secure in feeling that their personal and private life is theirs to keep
- trust that they are safe to make their own mistakes, choices and struggles on their life journey
- be a child, free from undue expectations or inappropriate burdens
- maintain good mental health.

In this section, we will be exploring how we as parents can create space for our children to confidently engage with these wonderful communities of people that God has planted us in. We will be looking at how we protect our children's sense of self, help them cope with the grittier side of ministry life, deal with congregational expectations and enable us as families to authentically lead while giving our children their own space to be themselves.

9

Protecting our children from exposure

I find the process of meeting new people fascinating. It usually goes something like this. You show up, and typically you have all the power. You can decide how the process goes. You can be friendly or shy. You can choose to talk a lot, or barely say anything. You can jump in and take the lead, or choose to sit back and watch.

When you first meet people, you are free from your past. No one has old stories of you or has any preconceived ideas of who you are or what you're like. They haven't heard bad rumours about you or any praises. You have a clean slate.

Eventually, you begin The Reveal. You ask questions and answer some. You choose when to give details and when to be vague. You decide how much vulnerability you are willing to show and how much time you are willing to invest in them. In places you stay or return to, you choose friends and then further decide who gets to see more and more aspects of your life, who gets to share in your pain and who gets to enter those private bits of your days and to listen to your thoughts.

This is the natural process of getting to know people. As individuals, we have the power to decide who to trust with our information and to make careful and wise calculations about what realm of influence and access each person has to us. We make mistakes, learn from them, adjust and continue. Private information is precious and needs to be respected and carefully portioned, even more so by us in church leadership.

Have you ever met someone who, upon hearing your name, says, 'Oh, yes! I've heard all about you.' Rarely do we think in response, 'What a relief! I feel completely comfortable and confident that all the information you have in your head is accurate and favourable. I feel more at ease now that you think you know all about me when I don't know you at all.' It's not always comfortable to experience that disproportionate sense of others feeling as if they know you and you not knowing them back.

When our children arrive at church and are met by people commenting on how wonderful their World Book Day costume looked, which they saw on social media, or congratulating them on their exam results, it can be hugely disorienting for them and can make them feel watched. It also robs them of the joy of sharing their own good news.

Do you remember when you found out you were pregnant or were finally approved for adoption? You probably took such delight in telling people your wonderful news. You loved the joy of seeing their faces, crying together with happiness, watching friends squeal or seeing your parents sob. Our children also have big news to share. They want to delight in telling people how they passed a swimming length, earned their next martial arts belt, had a birthday or passed their mock GCSEs with a higher mark than they expected. From the colour of their reception school uniform to which universities' open days they are going to, they are full of information they want to share. By *covering* their information, we enable them to share all the information themselves and to experience the relational and communal feeling of connection when they do.

If they are to grow in healthily forming relationships and to navigate them wisely, our children need to learn how to manage their own information. They need to learn the skills in how to wisely decide who can share information about them, what permissions to give others, and when and how to include people in their lives. When we protect our children's privacy, we give them that opportunity to be powerful to form their own relationships.

We can help create a healthy environment for our children's privacy in two ways: give them the safety of the shadows, and give them the gift of their own stories.

The safety of the shadows

As parents, we have a natural drive to introduce our children to our congregations. We want our congregations to know and love our children as we do. Most congregation members already have great affection and love for the leaders' children and have a sense of ownership in their well-being. They want our children to be well and to be welcomed. Often they are curious about our children, and out of genuine concern and care they ask questions about our children's school, their friends, their love interests and their personal achievements.

But when we share about our children on social media or in sermons, we put a spotlight on them and draw attention to them. We are saying, 'Watch this person.' Many of our children are too young to understand how that attention will impact them. If things are going great in their lives, they may not voice a dislike for it. But if things are not going so great, and they make some mistakes, change a bit or feel ashamed, they feel that the eyes of the congregation are on them, because they've been conditioned over the years that their personal lives are in the spotlight.

Through social media, in sermons and in our friendships and interactions, we give out our children's information a bit at a time. These bits of information may seem insignificant and innocuous to us, but they can become public and make our children feel that they are not in control of the natural process of choosing to know others and choosing to let others know them.

When we give out information about our children on social media, congregation members often leap on it and use it as jumping-off points for conversations with our children. Some of our children may have no idea we put up information about them on social media, so when strangers and casual acquaintances start talking to them about it, our children can feel powerless that their own information is being brought into the spotlight again and again.

There is safety in being hidden. We get to choose when we want to come out into the spotlight. We know how those we serve can seek and use information about us, for good and sometimes for manipulation. Sometimes *we* long for the safety and anonymity of the shadows. We can give that to our children, and we can protect it for them. We can make sure they are free to form their own relationships, to trust people with their own information and to decide who they want to let close.

Allow them not to be the public face of your family

Often our children's faces are splashed up on websites or slides in church. Occasionally we point out our children in church or ask them to join us on stage. The more we highlight our children and familiarise our congregations with them, the more our children can feel observed and watched.

If we want our children to be covered, we need to take steps to avoid pointing a spotlight on them. Talk about your children in general ('I have two great teenagers') rather than in detail ('Alexandra is 16 and an artist, and Rory is our wild, crazy and energetic 13-year-old'). The more you can cover your children, the more they can decide when and where they feel comfortable building their own relationships.

Be wary of what you put on social media

Any images, information or anecdotes we share on social media may be a source of information for curious and well-meaning congregation members. This can be difficult, as many of us love to share good things about our fabulous children, particularly if we have close family or friends who don't live near us. Some social media platforms allow us to select a smaller group of people to see certain posts. For instance, there is a 'family' tab we can choose on some social media platforms, so some posts will only be seen by a curated group of people.

Plan how to respond to enquiries and affirm it with your children

People will always want more and more information about your children. Most of the time, this interest is well-meaning and a sign of affection. Asking about their children is also a natural way of getting to know people.

It can be hard to know what to say in response, particularly when people ask questions like, 'How is your son doing in school?' or 'Do I see Sophie hanging out with Joe a lot? Is romance blossoming?' It may be worth thinking ahead about how you will respond, because 'No, she's not dating anyone' is as much of an answer as 'Yes, she is'. You might want to decide whether you say, 'We try hard to give her privacy and the freedom to develop her friendships without us trying to wriggle out info. You know how it is,' or, 'We are trying not to speculate. We just want her to feel comfortable being here. I'd appreciate it if you didn't ask her. I'm sure when she has something to tell us all, she will.'

If your teen doesn't show up for church, the inevitable question of where they are will be asked. Our desire to be honest can lead us to share too much information, such as, 'He's actually struggling with the church at the moment, so we've decided to let him stay home.

It's tricky. He's going through a bit of a rebellious phase right now, and we're trying to keep him on side.' Instead, we could guard his privacy and say, 'He's fine; he's just somewhere else today. How are you doing?'

There is a difference between being honest and ensuring that we enable our children to feel that their information is theirs. It can be useful to frame for our children how we respond whenever someone asks us a question about them, and invite them to refine our response. One church leader I know sat down with her children and said, 'When people ask me about you, I don't give them any informa-tion. I just say, "They're growing and getting on." Are you happy with that? Would you rather me encourage them to talk to you? How do you want me to answer questions about you?'

The gift of their own stories

We've all experienced it. There we are, hours into sermon prepar-ation, searching for an example of a situation or theological principle, when up floats a beautiful memory of our child that is the *perfect* illustration. There are so many excellent sermon illustrations that come up in family life, not to mention the funny stories that provide great icebreakers or some light relief in the middle of a sermon or meeting. We love our family, and they are with us a lot, so naturally we see God in lots of our circumstances and family stories – that perfect example of how a father-child relationship works that cracks open the parable of the prodigal son; a question our daughter asked; or a description of the way our children ministered to others. Our family stories are impactful and readily available, and telling them endears our family to the congregation. What could be wrong with it?

I heard once that one of the most common nightmares people have is being unexpectedly naked at work or school. Whatever your nightmares are, it appears that many of us have in common a sense of fear about being exposed, vulnerable, unprotected or uncovered. Our research has shown us that overwhelmingly, ministry children would prefer that their parents never tell stories about them in sermons. *No* church leader's child that I have ever been in contact with has genuinely said, 'I wish my parent told more stories about me to the congregation.' Why is that?

- It puts the spotlight on them and puts them at a disadvantage in relationships. Think about any icebreaker game you've played. It's usually about enabling everyone to share something *equally*, so everyone becomes comfortable with each other and grows in mutual discovery of each other. When we tell stories of our children, it instantly puts them at a disadvantage and into unequal relationships. Our children become known more than they know, with almost no possibility of catching up.

- Even if it is a good, positive story, it means that our children become a topic of conversation, and congregation members will mention it and bring it up a lot. It also adds pressure to our child to continue whatever the story was about for the sake of congregational expectations. If our child prayed for us once at home, and we told everyone, then he now can feel the pressure to be the 'prayer kid'. Children's teams may call on him more to pray. Church members may want to hear the story again, or they may be watching him during congregational prayer. Putting a spotlight even on great things can cause long-term exposure.

- It can introduce an unhelpful dynamic into your connection with your children. When your children are home with you, blissfully just living life, playing with you or sharing their questions and worries with you at night, they don't want to think that whatever is done in the privacy of their relationship with you may at some point be shared with the entire congregation. Many teenagers and young adults have told us that they began to distrust their private moments at home, because they began to wonder if some part of their parent's brain was always thinking, 'How can I use this for the sake of the church?' Our children need to know that their privacy is going to be *guarded* by us rather than *used* by us.

Stories belong to the people whom they are about. Our children have a lifetime of stories that belong to them. Some stories are private moments with family; others are their own experiences and thoughts that they've shared with us in trust. All those stories are theirs to tell, not ours.

A note about asking permission

At this point, many of us wonder, 'But what if I ask permission? Surely then I can use the stories.' On the one hand, yes. Asking permission to use our children's stories is better than not asking permission.

The downside to asking permission is that our children and teens cannot fully understand the consequences of saying yes. They cannot fully understand how stories about them could create within the congregation a sense of ownership over them. They cannot fully understand how their 'Yes' may impact how they feel about us or about their sense of safety in our church. They just don't know enough to give informed consent. Most of the time when we ask permission, our children just see the parent they love asking them for a favour, and they find it hard to say no. Our children don't want to let us down. They don't want to put us in the tough spot of having to struggle to find a different story. They may feel it would be selfish to say no. So they say yes.

I've known many church leaders who have tried to get around this by paying their children for their stories or asking them to think up a story they could use, but I always hear from the children that despite an initial sense of pride in helping their parent, a niggling bit of discomfort remains.

There is one approach that some have found successful, but for it to be useful it is important to use it rarely. This approach is to anonymise the story. After you decide that you want to use a story from your family, approach your child and ask if you can tell the story as if it happened to someone else: 'I know a family who was talking at home and the son said to the dad…' This can cover our children's identity and allow the story to be told. A word of warning, though: overuse of this method can lead to congregations twigging what you are doing. When this happens, the curtain gets ripped away, and a cacophony of stories that they remember from sermons past suddenly become about your family, even if they weren't. Any future stories that genuinely are about someone else can be assumed to be about your family. It can be a very useful approach, but use it sparingly.

When we get our children's privacy protection right, they will feel totally free to tell their own stories in church. They feel confident that the only information about them that people have is the information they themselves have given, and they can delight in sharing it with joy. Let's give this gift of privacy to our children so they can thrive in relationships that they themselves build.

10

Living in the goldfish bowl: dealing with congregational expectations

Dealing with the expectations of the congregation can be extremely difficult. We can sometimes feel as if we're trying to navigate a complicated maze, looking for the right combination of paths that will lead towards a balance between doing what we feel called to do and doing what our congregations expect us to do. It can be an exhausting endeavour.

We can find that many of our congregation members have expectations for our family life. They expect we will put the church first, that our spouse will be heavily involved in the church or that our children will behave beautifully and engage with the service and events. They can even apply a vague pressure of expectation to *how* we parent: what behaviours we permit or restrict, what choices we allow our children to make in their everyday lives and how we as a family interact on a Sunday.

When our children live under the pressure of expectation, they stop feeling able to engage with the church as themselves and instead feel they have to create a 'church leader's child' persona that they can grow to resent. If we want our children to feel comfortable to be themselves in this community, to authentically create relationships and to invest in serving the church and in exploring their faith alongside others, then we need to create a way for them to thrive free from the pressure of congregational expectation.

Discovering our congregation's expectations is never straightforward. It is a rare church that articulates during the induction process, 'Welcome! We look forward to seeing your spouse at three-quarters of all church events, and we anticipate their leadership within children's ministry or outreach community pastoral care. We expect your children to sit still and quietly, to never run and to make moral and highly conservative decisions in their personal lives, as well as to be publicly and adorably "Christian", serving as models for other children and teens.'

Most of us discover the congregation's expectations through their unguarded expressions and comments in casual conversations. These indications can make us feel unsure of our choices and hyper-aware of the subtle signs people use to communicate their preferences to us. We begin to have all sorts of questions: is this level of baby noise okay in this service? What about a teenager on a gadget? Should my nine-year-old be attending the after-school club? Can I walk around the sides of the church with a toddler?

Our children also notice and internalise the expectations that they sense the congregation is communicating to them. For their sakes, and for ours, it is helpful to determine how we want to approach these expectations, so we can enable ourselves and our families to be authentic and not feel forced into a shape we haven't chosen.

Be bold to be the ordinary you

I believe the best way to serve the church and our family's mental, emotional and spiritual health is for us to decide who we are as a family, commit to living that well and communicate those values and choices respectfully to our communities.

It may be helpful to answer questions like these:

- What kind of family do we feel called to be in this church?
- Who are we supposed to be in this community?
- What is our children's role within this church?
- What are healthy church expectations for our children and what are harmful ones we need to shield them from?
- How do we want to parent in this goldfish bowl of leadership?

Wanting to model the perfect family isn't the position that will make our families thrive. I don't know anyone working in mental healthcare who would advocate striving for perfection as an approach that creates a balanced and beneficial vision for our families.

So what do we do? Let's first look at that inescapable goldfish bowl we live in. People *are* watching us. But we sometimes misinterpret *why*. We feel as if they are watching and judging us because they want us to be perfect or because they have firm views of what we *should* do and are measuring us up. While a few may have that motivation, the vast majority are watching for a completely different reason: to see a Christian family interacting with each other right in front of them.

Before the Industrial Revolution, most people parented in public. They had their children and teenagers with them on the farm, at the forge and in the bakery and other shops. Family life and work life were much more integrated, and people lived near each other in villages or towns. They lived in extended family groups, with multiple families living close together in one home or area. Their friends, family and neighbours were the same ones throughout their lives. People learned how to parent from doing it together, side by side, in front of each other.

In our modern society, people have few opportunities to see what Christian family life truly looks like. Our families seem to be so isolated from each other. There are few places where we can see people we respect going about parenting their own children. In the typical workplace, people don't see their colleagues or bosses parenting their teen through a rebellious phase or playing on the floor with their toddler. This level of intimacy among others is mostly hidden from us nowadays. But in the church setting, people do have the opportunity to watch us parent. They may watch not necessarily because they want to disapprove or judge, but because they genuinely want to see what it looks like for a godly family to parent. They are looking for answers to their own questions, such as, 'How do I help my kid meet and know God?', 'How do I help my kid engage in church?' and 'Should I expect my child to come to church, and what does that look like?'

Parents want people to parent alongside them. They want to learn how to do the spiritual side of parenting and how to bring their faith into their parenting choices. We, as church leaders, help them with all the other areas of how faith affects their lives, and now they are looking for us to wade into helping them with parenting as well.

They are watching, because our lives make them reflect on their own. Even those who have adult children, or those who do not have children, still watch. They still reflect. By living our regular lives, we are creating windows into what life with God looks like in our family. If we feel the pressure to make our lives look perfect, then we are telling our congregations that perfection in the family is what God expects. And I know that isn't the message we want to give out.

Instead, give your congregation the message that you and your family are on a journey, just like any other family. Whatever values you have as a family, and however you're muddling through to figure it all out, *be bold to be you, as imperfect and in-the-middle as you are.*

It is unrealistic for *any* parent to think, 'I totally have this figured out, and parenting is going exactly as I want it to go.' It is unfair for us to place this great pressure upon ourselves. We cannot and should not have to be the parenting expert of the church. People older than us who have done all their parenting may have opinions on how we should do it. People who are our peers may be looking for help. Younger people may be watching to learn from us. It is so easy to take all these observations, expectations and opinions, and to conclude, 'I have to become the model for well-thought-out Christian parenting.'

It's not true. You are a parent, figuring out your journey just like everyone else. You have successes and experiments, and things that fall through the cracks because you can't do everything. It's okay. One of the best gifts you can give yourself, your kids and your congregation is the gift of being okay with just being you in your own church.

Be the model of ordinary. Be the model of being kind to yourself as you figure it out. Be the model of a gracious family, figuring it out and being grateful for the community around you. By being ordinary, you permit other people to be ordinary too.

The power of framing

What is the key to being confident to parent our children, to model authentic family life without too much exposure for our kids and to free our family from living in response to congregational expectation? The answer is simple. And you already know what it is: framing.

In chapter 3, we talked about the importance of framing. Framing is simply explaining to others what they are looking at, so they can understand the situation and know how to engage with it. Since we want our congregations and our children to understand our parenting choices, then we need to frame those choices for them.

The power of framing for your congregation

Create an understanding of your approach

As church leaders we have many opportunities to talk about our families, whether during our introduction to a congregation, in a sermon, in the church newsletter or in our bio on the church website. These can be great places to frame our parenting values for our congregations.

In whichever place you choose to do so, frame your values in your own words and express them from your heart. Let them sound like you. Look at these examples from church leaders who have expressed their parenting approach to their congregation in their own way. Notice that each one creates a sense of imperfection in a few short sentences:

> We are parents on the journey of trying to help our children grow in finding their path every day and in walking with God along the way. We make a lot of mistakes, but we are figuring it out, just as you are. We love that we have a church community to be family in, and that you love and support us as we try!

* * *

> We have no idea what we are doing, but we love the adventure of figuring it out. The best support you can give us is not advice but more encouragement! We are so grateful to have you in our lives.

* * *

It is so great to be part of a community that wants to see our children thrive as much as we do. We are so grateful to be parenting our children in a place that welcomes and creates space for our children to be just who they are, without putting any pressure on them to be anyone else.

These examples represent the heart approaches of *those* families. You may like their statements or you may reject them completely. The important thing is that you grow to know what *your* statement is. When you feel confident enough to frame your statement for your congregation, then you will have created space for yourself and your family to be who you are, not who you think the congregation wants you to be.

'You know how it is'

I grew up being friends with our church leader's child, and I vividly remember how her mum, Judy, would use one phrase to wipe away all expectations of perfection and at the same time invite people to understand and identify with her: 'You know how it is.'

So often I found myself in church leadership feeling the need to apologise for not living up to the unspoken – and often totally imagined – expectations that I assumed the congregation had of me. I would apologise for a slightly messy lounge, for my child making tiny noises, for being late when I had to change clothes for the third time due to child bodily fluids – until I remembered Judy.

I don't remember Judy agonising and apologising: I simply remember her exuding her values and inviting people to understand. Rather than apologising for her house looking a mess because her daughter and I were playing, she would say, 'Welcome to our home. Come on into the kitchen. Heather and Rachel are having a great adventure in the lounge.' Then she would wink a bit and say with loads of charm, 'You know how it is.'

Rather than apologising and stumbling over herself to say, 'This is unacceptable, I know. I should have a perfect house and always be early,' her attitude was, 'Ugh, family life is the same everywhere. You know exactly what I'm feeling now, and I love that I can count on you to understand.' She would do this for almost everything. If she showed up late to some event, she would say, 'Hi, everyone. It's great to get here finally. I had to pick up a costume for tomorrow at school. You know how it is.' I could go on. Every time, people would nod and smile and sometimes tell their own stories. She would create a community of understanding parents simply by assuming they would be.

I thought the phrase was genius, and I borrow it all the time. That doesn't mean I never apologise, but the addition of the phrase 'You know how it is' frames for others that my life is like theirs, and it gives me, and them, permission to support and understand as we do family life together.

Responding to congregational advice, opinions and complaints

People will approach you about your parenting choices and your children's behaviour, attitudes, clothes and general existence. Before they do, it's worth thinking through how you want to respond. Your reply is not just for your own personal peace, but also for your children's. How you respond speaks volumes to your children, and it gives you an opportunity to model for them how to live and respond when people are watching.

It can be helpful to know that most people who have a comment for us have the best intentions at heart. If we begin to perceive that every suggestion, comment and piece of advice shared with us is a vicious judgement of our parenting skills, we will crumble. Assume the best of all those who want to say something to you. Assume that they love you and want the best for you and that, for some reason, they think their comment is a positive thing. When we assume a good intention, we can phrase a response to that *intention* rather than to the actual comment that comes out of their mouths.

When people come up and offer unsolicited advice, feel free to use a prepared phrase, and then get out of the conversation. Your phrase could be something like this: 'I'm sure we'll figure it out. I'll add that to the list of things to ponder. Every child is different, and we are experimenting with lots of ways.' This communicates to the person: 'I'm not committing to doing anything you are saying, but I'm reminding you that parenting takes time and adjustment, so don't expect anything to change soon. But thanks for loving me.'

If you are feeling bold, you can help them see how they *can* help you, because unsolicited advice usually doesn't: 'Yes, I have heard of that approach before, but right now we are trying this. Do you know what would help us, though? Babysitting.' Or, 'What a great idea! I'd love to do that. Would you mind walking with my toddler after church so I can try that?'

Sometimes you can respond by framing one of your family's values:

Yes, I can understand how my two-year-old walking up to her mum while she's leading the service may be distracting. I so appreciate your grace and patience. We think it's really important that all children, not just ours, feel welcome and comfortable at church, and right now she is too young to understand why her mum is ignoring her while being right there. We thought we'd try this approach and see if it works. We've never parented this particular kid through this season before, so I'm sorry if it's distracting for you. We are working on it, but it might not be fixed soon.

If you are feeling super generous, you can add in:

And if more families join, as we hope they will, it will probably get even more distracting. How can I help you find space that enables you to meet with God, while also creating space for all families to come and not feel unwelcome to be themselves? Both are important, and if you aren't able to connect with God, that's important to address too.

There's a confidence that comes with knowing how you want to respond, rather than just feeling frustrated and wanting to scream, 'I'm exhausted and this kid won't stop touching me. The fact that we are here at all is a miracle. Just applaud my extraordinary self-control and leave me alone, please.'

The power of framing for your children

Non-church leaders' children have normal faith journeys, which are hidden and personal. When they attend church or children's ministry, they blend together with the many other children in the room. Some weeks they are disconnected; others they are thoughtful. They go through seasons both of nightmare behaviour and of keen interest and connection with God. They make mistakes and decisions. They may drift away, or they may discover a passion for ministry. Their journeys are their own, and their leaders support them along the way and celebrate them as they reach milestones and transitions.

Church leaders' children, on the other hand, do *not* have normal faith journeys. Theirs can be quite public, unfortunately. And to make matters more difficult, the watching congregation often also has expectations of them. Our children are expected to have faith, to possess better knowledge of the Bible than others and to be naturally willing to lead. They are expected to love God and to behave well. Their journeys with God are watched, judged and exposed.

As church leaders, we also have our own unspoken expectations of our children, and sometimes we don't even know we have them. For instance, we might expect our children to participate fully in church events or to show other kids how to respond to God. We may be deeply embarrassed if it's *our* six-year-old running around and refusing to engage in the all-age prayer activity. Sometimes we can feel as if the congregation uses our children's spirituality and faith to judge *us*, and sometimes we use it to judge ourselves too. We can all watch our children and ask ourselves, 'Is my worth as a church leader based on how Christian my children are?'

Children can feel the weight of all these expectations, even if no one articulates them. It can be so helpful to discuss these with our children proactively. By doing so, we can give them permission to be themselves in the places where they're struggling with expectations and needing to hear our affirmation. We can also clear up any confusion about situations they may find themselves in. Our children sometimes need us to say:

> I'm your parent and so it's my job, not anyone else's, to decide what is okay for you to do and not do at church. There will always be people in life who have opinions about what you should do. But your job is to decide between you and God what is right. And when you can't decide, you can look to me as your parent to see where your boundaries and yeses are. Other people's views don't get to be part of your choices. If other people say things to you that you feel are unfair, then I'd like to know. You are a kid like everyone else's kid, and it's my job to help you be free to be you.

You may need to be proactive in affirming their choices too: 'I notice that you wanted to sit down during worship. I'm okay with that as long as you are finding your own way of connecting with God.'

Sometimes when we choose to be proactive, we expose our own lack of surety in what our values are for any given situation. One of the most important parts of this particular journey of ours is growing our confidence to personally parent our children for faith and to coach them on their spiritual journey at home and at church. All parents are figuring this out as they go along, but we can feel particularly exposed when we're figuring this out as the church leader's family.

The final section, 'Empowered', is all about helping our kids along their faith journey, so that we can feel confident in helping our children meet and know God for themselves, regardless of what the congregation thinks.

A note on discipline

It can be excruciating to feel that people are judging our parenting. As soon as we begin to discipline in front of others, we feel as if our very character is on display. We imagine the unspoken questions behind their looks: Will you yell at them? Will they obey? What will you do if they don't? How will you get them to do what you say? Are you going to let them get away with that? Are you someone who has their respect?

Even when we're with the friendliest of people, whether work colleagues, supervisors or members of the congregation, we feel pressure parenting in front of them. One reason for this pressure is the fact that we're attempting to discipline *in our work location*. Most congregation members don't understand how awkward this is. They haven't had their toddlers dropped off at their work location for the day and been expected to complete their job with excellence while perfectly controlling themselves and their roaming children.

All that pressure can sometimes push us into making parenting decisions based on what we think other people want us to do, rather than what we feel is right. Here are a few thoughts on handling discipline for our children when others are around.

Check what you are disciplining for

Our children can quickly become resentful of us, the church and the congregation when they feel they are subject to unfairness for the sake of looking perfect to others. This can happen when we are embarrassed by their actions and slam down discipline, whether it's for running around after church, saying something cheeky or behaving like the disengaged kid rather than the super keen kid. If we discipline out of embarrassment or because of how we think we appear to others, then we are setting up our children to feel we are picking on them because of their status.

When we simply choose to be the same parent with the same rules when we are at home and when we are in 'the goldfish bowl' at church, we will go a long way towards creating normality for our children. So before we discipline our children, we need to take a moment and ask ourselves, 'Am I disciplining because of my values or because I'm embarrassed?'

Cover your children's privacy by disciplining in private

If we want our children to feel covered and protected from embarrassment and judgement, then *how* and *when* we discipline our children become important. No one, including adults, likes being told off in front of others. It is shameful and humiliating, especially for high-profile children who are being watched. One of the greatest gifts we can give our children is guarding their privacy when it comes to their mistakes and their discipline.

When our children are in trouble, calling them over to have a whispered 'conversation' in front of people can still put a huge spotlight on them. Given that a lot of our discipline can happen when congregation members are around, it is important that we find a pattern of creating private space in which to discipline.

Our children will feel covered and safe when they know that if we do tell them off or spell out consequences for their bad behaviour, we will *never* do so publicly. Some church leaders calmly call their children over by saying, 'Can I have a word?', or by merely whispering, 'Let's chat outside now, please.' Then both of them pop out of the room or walk around the corner and have their chat. Understandably this may be hard to do with under-fives, so the approach with them may look different for each of us. But if we start with the principle of protecting our child's privacy, we can find safe, private locations for them to serve out their consequences without too much exposure.

As our children grow older and we create new patterns of discipline, they can continue to grow in trust that we will keep their learning journeys private. They will be assured that we won't discipline in public or talk about or use their mistakes as illustrations or anecdotes in humorous stories. They can feel safe to be themselves and go on their learning journeys in private, just as we all do. And when they feel safe, they can rest their hearts and engage with our church communities as themselves.

11

Navigating confidentiality

Over the past few decades, more and more research has shown that consistent multigenerational relationships within a church are of significant importance. These relationships greatly support and reinforce the spiritual growth and development of children and young people. Fuller Youth Institute showed that, while there are many factors to children's faith developments, creating and sustaining a 'sticky web' of multigenerational relationships is essential in helping children lock into faith and church community.[13]

This 'sticky web' includes worshipping together as an all-age community, extends to the importance of key individual relationships with members of the congregation and goes in all directions. Children and teens' relationships with those younger than them are vital, as well as ones with peers and adults. Fuller Youth Institute's recommendations echo other secular social scientists and suggest that every child or teen would greatly benefit from having five significant adults proactively and consistently involved in being a caring, trusted, interested presence in their life.

This 'sticky web' creates a community that believes in our children, that needs them and that is needed by them. These significant adults create windows for our children to see the variety of faith journeys people go on, and they equip and empower our children to be powerful in ministry. As church leaders, we are positioned beautifully to provide these opportunities for our children and their faith journeys.

We can do this in two ways: foster positive relationships with others, and teach the values for holding confidentiality.

Foster positive relationships with others

In our normal jobs, we are responsible for the pastoral care of a large number of people. Our congregants welcome us to walk alongside them through deaths, births, struggles, hopes lost and callings found. It is our honour and privilege when they invite us into these vulnerable areas of their lives, and we are humbled by the experience. As part of our job as church leaders, we learn to cope with the weight of the confidential information entrusted to us. We know a lot about those we serve, but we must not share all we know.

If we want our children to have good, open relationships with the people we serve in our congregations, especially with those who can form a 'sticky web' around them, then we need to help our children see people from God's perspective. We can do this by speaking about people in ways that are gracious and that will foster and maintain our children's relationships with them. Here are a few ways to do that.

Speak well of the congregation

God loves our people, all our people, even the most grumpy, obstructionist, aggressive person in our teams or congregations, and so we can speak well of them in front of our children. One couple in church leadership made it a rule to only have good things to say about the congregation in front of their children, so that their children would see the good in others and feel safe at church. And their children did. They also grew to speak of others using the same language of grace that their parents had demonstrated to them over the years.

Another church leader had worked in a church with much internal conflict. He and his wife chose to explain any conflict their children became aware of with the view of preserving and encouraging their children's emotional connection and comfortableness with the people involved. They felt it was important that whatever conflict they themselves were experiencing would not be a catalyst to push their children out of the church community. And because of their choice, it didn't.

Whether it's talking about people, conflict or situations you've observed, be aware that our children are listening for clues from us about how to think and feel about the community they are embedded in. If we give them positive, honouring words about our people and the church, we help our children preserve their positive relationships with members of the congregations, especially with those special people who are a part of their 'sticky web'.

Make your debriefings private

Many of us need to have a good debrief after events, services and meetings. Sometimes we debrief to communicate with our spouses or friends, to process what we think or to just remember everything that happened that day. Whether or not we have a partner, it's important to think through how we debrief.

If we want our children to view members of the congregation with grace, joy and an expectation of positivity, we need to plan how to have our debriefings away from our children and out of their hearing. Some church leaders plan an afternoon movie every Sunday, where the children get to pick a movie and watch with popcorn while mum and dad talk in the kitchen and then join in when they are done. Another church leader I know sends texts to his partner throughout the day, creating an 'ask me about' list for the two of them to use later when they have time and when the kids are out or asleep. Other people I know debrief on the phone with a friend or partner during the commute/walk home, as long as the children aren't with them.

Remember, the goal is for children and teens to learn to see people as loved by God and to see a community they *want* to be a part of. That doesn't mean lying to them; it means giving them the security that non-church leaders' children have, which is in *not* knowing the 'inside scoop' on everyone's life.

When we choose to debrief away from our children, we are preserving their journey of learning about people in the congregation on their own terms. This doesn't mean that they will spend a lifetime thinking that people in the church are perfect – that is fairly impossible. It just means that as people choose to share their stories and thoughts with our children, we are there to help them know what to do with all that information, rather than us being the source of much of that information.

Anonymise personal information

It is important to share about our days and tell our children what is going on in our lives. As a parent in ministry, our children can learn so much from us about how we see, think and feel about those on our teams and those we lead. They can learn where God is in situations and conflicts, what we're still trying to figure out, when we're lost or doubting and how we're making decisions.

This kind of openness is essential, not just to build a connection with our children but also to help them learn how ministry and leadership work and how we emotionally and spiritually navigate it. So, yes, tell stories. Yes, create windows into your life. Yes, frame situations. Just protect people's privacy when you do it. Anonymise other people's information so that when you speak with your children, your story's focus is on you and what you are communicating, rather than on specific people and their private information.

Avoid telling your story like this:

> I was visiting Joan today in hospital. Do you know Joan? John and Sarah's mum? Well, she's in there being investigated for cervical cancer. It's just awful. She's really upset, and the kids are a mess too. Her condition is not looking good. She wants to talk about who might take her kids if this turns out to be fatal. So awful.

Choose, instead, to tell your story in a way that preserves people's privacy:

> I feel like my soul is tired. I was visiting someone in hospital, and she thinks she may die. This person has children, so we had to discuss tough details like where the kids might go if she dies and other things. It breaks my heart. I want God to heal her, so that her family won't have to walk this. And yet I also know that God is with her right where she is. I have so many emotions. When I'm there, I'm just focused on making her laugh and on listening to what she wants to say, but when I come home, it all hits me. I spent most of my shower asking God for wisdom on how to help her.

In both examples, you are talking about your experience. The first example draws our children's attention to people they know, to children they know and may or may not like, and to a really difficult and immediate situation their friends may or may not be in. When our children hear this version of the story, they want to deal with the immediacy of the situation rather than focusing on learning from or connecting with us. The second example allows space for our children to have compassion for the family and hear how you are feeling and coping with knowing that information. By anonymising the private information when you talk about it with the kids, you can preserve your children's independence from owning the problem while still enabling their compassionate response.

Teach the values for holding confidentiality

Our children don't only overhear confidential information at home; they also pick up private information when they are in the midst of the congregation at church and when they are together with their peers in youth group. When our children hear or overhear confidential information, it can put them in very difficult positions, emotionally, mentally and spiritually. We need to protect our children in the awkward and uncomfortable position of holding other people's confidential information.

How can we support and equip our children to respond when they encounter private pastoral information or not-yet-released church plans? How can we help our children thrive when they are party to secrets and to levels of confidentiality that pop up within the church context they live in? How can we still foster and encourage those important relationships in our children's lives, the ones that create 'sticky webs', when they've heard confidential information about those congregants?

The answer is twofold. We can teach our children a foundation of values they can understand and can apply to all situations involving confidentiality, and we can model what that foundation looks like in our own lives. In that way, when our children encounter specific instances involving confidentiality, they will have values-based tools to use, as well as having our own lives as examples of how to apply those tools to the situation at hand.

It can be helpful to start talking with our children about the larger values that underlie and form our responses to confidentiality. It is most helpful to discuss these values before an actual situation arises, so they are in place when our children need them. By equipping our children with these, and any others you think of, our children can make wise decisions about handling information. Here are a few values to consider teaching:

- *Protect people's information* – 'One of the ways we protect people is by protecting their hearts, and we can do that by protecting the information that they entrust to us. Can you please be part of the team that protects their heart by not sharing their information with others? Since we both know the information, if you have any questions or concerns, please feel free to chat about it with me.'

- *Avoid gossip* – 'It can feel powerful to know something that others don't know. It can make you feel important because you have knowledge that others don't have. It can make you feel popular because people like hearing things that they don't know or shouldn't know. But using others to feel those things is wrong. God doesn't like gossip, because it treats other people as things to be used rather than as his precious children to protect.'

- *Let other people own their stories* – 'When something happens to you, you own it. It happened to you, and you can choose whom to share that with or whom not to share it with. I, as your parent, will protect that and support that. But we as a family also choose to protect and support that for everyone. It's our job to protect others' stories for them, and that's a big task.'

- *Keep no secrets between us* – 'God put us in family for lots of reasons. One of those reasons is so that I can help you in all your life. That means I am a safe person for you to share things with, things that are on your heart. When we hear information about others, we can wonder what to do with it. Sometimes people want us to keep their secrets. It's my job to help you figure out how to do that well, and what is a safe secret to keep and what isn't. That means I don't want you to say yes if someone says not to tell me something.'

When we free our children from the responsibility and stress of holding confidential information, we can free them to invest in the relationships that they build with congregation members around them. We can empower their 'sticky web' of relationships that will enable them to embed in church and be surrounded by affirming relationships. We can also lay down a healthy foundation of values for them, so that as they are trusted with information through their relationships, or are accidentally party to additional information based on their proximity to us, they know how to healthily and lightly handle that responsibility.

12

Tricky bits: freeing our children to build close relationships

Covered: free to form deep relationships

One of the main reasons for covering our children is so they can be free to form healthy and supportive relationships within our church community. God created us all for close relationship with him and with others. If any of us feel limited in our ability to have people truly walk alongside us, then that lack can fester into intense loneliness, isolation or depression.

Within my very close relationships, I feel free to share everything, including what I adore about my child and the intimate details of my life and ministry. That is the joy of having close family and friends.

We want our children to have that too – to have those people around them with whom they can openly talk and laugh and share anything and everything. Those relationships are vital to their growth as individuals. Our children need to feel free to create relationships and to establish the openness and honesty with specific friends that enable them to have the love and support they need as people, and as children of church leaders.

We can help our children and teens in two ways: create windows into the importance of no-holds-barred friendship, and enable and empower your children to establish their own group of friends with whom they can feel safe.

Create windows

Your children may not know how you feel about friendship. It would be helpful every once in a while to create a window into your journey of friendship, especially as a church leader. You may say:

> I'm going to call Annie. I'm thinking something through, and I want to be able to say everything I'm feeling and thinking without worrying about it getting around. I trust Annie, and I value her wisdom and input. And she makes me laugh.

Or:

> I love that no matter where we go, Susie and James and Jo and Elliott are always there when I want to chat or get wisdom. I know it's hard when we move, to make new friends and start over in a new church community. That's why I love how these four people always make our friendship work no matter where we live. I need them in my life.

When our children can see and hear how friendships are essential to our hearts, they can feel validated that they need friendships too.

It is worth remembering that these long-term relationships are filled with friends and family who know us and our children well, and who become the powerful members of our children's 'sticky web' of intergenerational relationships. These friends and family continually show our children that the church is much bigger than the one place they attend.

Enable and empower

Children's lives tend to be centred on the now, and they have a small set of friends at church or school who are a part of that. Our children haven't had the luxury of 15 years of building up adult friendships, or years of experience in growing and maintaining long-distance friendships. They simply have these friends, and they have them now.

If we want our children to have the kind of deep relationships that bring us life and support, then we need to free them to talk about *everything* with their friends. And that includes giving them permission to talk about *us*. We loom large in our children's home and church life, and so our children need to be able to talk about how they feel about us and how they feel about being a church leader's child. Particularly as teens, connection with others is vital, and some of that connecting is processing their feelings about us and the church.

That realisation can make us slightly uncomfortable, because we are aware that we are more relaxed at home than we are at work. We dance in the lounge in a way that embarrasses our teens. We sing in the kitchen. We get cranky when someone touches the project we're working on. The intimate, unguarded moments of family life belong to us *and* to our children, so if they tell their friends at church about us, it can make us feel a bit exposed.

But if we say, 'You can't talk about me with your friends,' then we are setting them up either to disobey us or to hold themselves back from their friends. We are asking them to choose one or the other. Neither option is good.

Instead, let's give our children permission to talk about us to their close friends, and let's use the opportunity to instruct them about real relationship. We can talk about how trustworthy friends guard our privacy, just as we are supposed to guard theirs. Share with them, for example by saying:

It's hard being the church leader, and there are bits of my life that I only share with some family and friends whom I trust to protect my private information. I also know that it can be hard for you to be a child of a church leader. And just as I have some friends I can freely talk to about everything, I know you need friends like that too. There will be times when you will need to talk with trusted people about how you feel about us, your mum and dad. I get that! I needed that when I was your age too. Could I just ask that as you pick friends, would you make sure that they will be really faithful to guard your privacy? I know that no one's perfect, and that sometimes we miscalculate who is trustworthy and who is not; I'm okay with that. I don't want you just telling everyone about our private home life. But some trustworthy friends who guard and take care of you? Absolutely, feel free.

Brace yourself, because sometimes your children's friends aren't as rock solid as they thought, and that's okay. Our children can go on that journey, knowing that you support them in finding relationships where they can share all their thoughts and feelings.

When we show our children that church can be a place of support and connection, even if we keep some things private, we can help them feel safe and connected to the wider church and learn how to benefit from its encouragement and ministry. When we let our children know that deep friendship is important to us and that it's okay for it to be important to them, they can feel free to pursue friendship for themselves. When we give them permission to share all, they can have people who deeply understand them and hold their hearts well.

IV

Empowered

13

The strength of empowering our children's faith

One of the greatest joys of being a parent is helping our children grow to love God and follow him. We yearn for our children to develop the kind of deep relationship with God that will anchor them as they move into young adulthood, the kind of deep faith that will enable them to follow God all the days of their lives, no matter what their futures hold. We desperately want this for our children, yet we know that *we* can't make it happen for them. Ultimately, they must choose it for themselves.

One of the greatest fears we can have as parents is knowing that we cannot guarantee the outcome of our efforts to lead our children to deep faith in God. A recent study has examined the factors that contribute to our children's decision to walk in faith or to walk away from faith,[14] and the findings are significant. The research found that one of the most important factors in whether a church leader's child continues in, or walks away from, faith is how *empowered* the child feels to go on their own faith journey. In other words, children are more likely to continue in faith if they feel *empowered* to be free to make their own faith choices and to own their connection with God. If they do, their commitment will not be for the sake of their parents or the performance of the congregation, but for themselves.

When we *empower* our children to embark on their own faith journeys, they can:

- know they are entrusted to go on their own adventure with God, and we will be cheering them on
- be encouraged to discover daily what life with God looks like for them
- play the part they feel called to play in the body of Christ
- feel the strength and joy of being an ordinary member of a congregation, able to make mistakes and be lifted up by others.

Figuring out how to freely and graciously *empower* our children's faith journeys means developing skills and tools to use as we walk alongside and encourage them. This section will help us explore what that means in practice. We will look at the Key Tools we need as parents to help our children discover God in their everyday life, and we will also look at how we can help our children connect with God in church and find their place within it.

14

Helping our children meet and know God in everyday life

Empowered

In scripture we can see several levels of children's discipleship: first, what happens at home with parents, and then the wider community of the church, which wraps around parents. Parents provide the sense of God in daily life and walk alongside their children in their faith journeys. The church becomes a place of support, love and challenge, and it creates a sense of team for our families and children as they become part of the greater body of Christ.

The first level of discipleship for our children is us, their parents. This is not because we are church leaders, not because of the theological knowledge we have and not because of the level of influence we have within the church. It is because we are their parents. We can offer our children something the church can't: everyday access to someone who loves them, loves God and is willing to help them see who God is in the everyday.

Deuteronomy 6:5-9 makes it clear that the design for children and teens' discipleship is to be wrapped up in the ordinary, boring bits of life:

> Love the Lord your God with all your heart and with all your
> soul and with all your strength. These commandments that
> I give you today are to be on your hearts. Impress them on your
> children. Talk about them when you sit at home and when you
> walk along the road, when you lie down and when you get up.
> Tie them as symbols on your hands and bind them on your
> foreheads. Write them on the door-frames of your houses and
> on your gates.
>
> DEUTERONOMY 6:5–9 (NIV)

Children's discipleship happens in these ordinary moments because
that's where God's power, strength, love, grace and joy are. We want
our children to see and know him there. Since parents and carers
are the ones who walk alongside their children in those places and
times, they are the ones best suited to do the discipling.

Parents and carers have, on average, between 2,000 and 3,000 hours
per year of ordinary time with their children to help them on their
journey with God. These hours are often broken down into smaller
bits of time throughout the day: the 20 minutes when everyone is
eating breakfast and getting ready; the journey to school; the time
making tea or preparing a meal; the 15 minutes of bedtime snuggles;
the time spent at the supermarket or making other trips here and
there; and the hanging-out time with one child while waiting for
the other one's swimming lesson to be done. Parents have as much
ordinary time *in two weeks* with their children as *one year's* worth
of Sunday services.[15] Your time at home with your children is much
more powerful than your children's time at church.

If we are to see our children grow in their connection with God,
rather than just in their understanding and head knowledge of God,
then we can use those tiny bits of time to help our children find an
authentic faith and a walk with God in their everyday. There are five
main tools that we as parents can use to do this well.

The five Key Tools

I remember the worst moving day I ever had. We were moving house yet again for a new ministry post, and I had taken upon myself the job of reconstructing the many pieces of flat-pack furniture we own. I love that job – it makes me feel epic and productive – so I was looking forward to an afternoon of building achievements. I had laid out all the pieces of one of my chairs, along with all the screws and connectors, and then I looked for the most important part: the Allen key that would enable me to put it all together. It wasn't there. I checked everywhere – under boxes, in our toolboxes and in my husband's jacket pockets. It was nowhere. 'That's fine,' I thought. 'It can't be that hard. I'll just use something else.'

With this decision began the most frustrating afternoon of my life. I tried a screwdriver, but it was either too big, too small or not grippy enough to stay in that little hexagonal socket. I tried holding the sides with pliers, but they slipped off. I tried hammering the connector in, but it wouldn't budge and the wood started to crack. Despite my enormous effort, without the right tool I couldn't achieve what I wanted. After three hours of impressive effort, sweating and once genuinely praying, I gave in and went to our local hardware shop to buy a set of Allen keys. After that, the furniture virtually built itself. When you use the right tool, the effort required is minimal, because the tool is specifically designed to be effective for the task at hand.

God set up children's discipleship to have a family at its core, wrapped around by the church. As church leaders and parents, we can become comfortable and proficient with the tools we need to help our children's journey of faith at home, as well as to encourage and support our children to find their place in church. Our children need proactive *parents* doing the things that only *parents* are perfectly positioned for.

The rest of this chapter gives a brief overview of some of the principles covered in *Parenting Children for a Life of Faith* (BRF, 2018) and in the Parenting for Faith course.[16] Those of you who have read the book or done the course may therefore want to skip to the next chapter, or continue reading for a quick refresher. If this is new to you, I'd like to briefly cover the Key Tools we can use to parent for faith at home in the everyday, using our position as parents to enable our children to develop their own connection with God.

1 Creating Windows

In chapter 3, we explored the idea of Creating Windows. This tool is particularly important to church leaders as parents because of the amount of time our children see us engaging in corporate expressions of faith. Most of what we lead within the church is corporate. We pray together, read the Bible together, sing worship songs together, talk together and participate in rituals and sacraments together. We show our children how we engage with corporate worship, then we turn to them and say, 'You can have a one-to-one personal connection to God.' Often, the only experiences they have of encountering God are corporate, so our children only know how to connect to God using all the corporate tools we give them. But that isn't how people learn how to have relationships.

One of the ways people learn to relate to others is by observation. Whether it is watching others' friendships or seeing how you and your spouse relate to each other, our children learn what life can be like by looking into the lives of others and trying it for themselves. The problem is that so often our relationship with God is private and hidden, so our children can't look and learn. All they might see of our relationship with God is through our leadership within the church, which leaves us displaying only the corporate model to our children.

Our children need to see what an authentic, up-and-down, in-the-good-times-and-dry-times relationship with God looks like at home in the ordinary everyday, not just publicly in church leadership. They need to see how to handle disappointment and doubt, fear and joy, and hope and uncertainty, and to know where God is in all of that.

We can give our children a great gift by choosing to create windows into our lives with God, strategically. We don't have to fling open the doors and show them everything. We simply need to open windows for them to see through, so they can learn what life with God is like. For example, we could leave our study door open a crack so that our children can see us reading the Bible, let them hear us wrestling with a tough theological issue or with feeling dry with God, or let them be around us as we pray and worship. From big issues to little thoughts, as we create windows into our life with God, our children will be able to see what it can be like and they can try it for themselves. If you want to be reminded of this tool, you can refresh yourself on page 44.

2 Framing

The second tool is Framing, and we also talked about this one in chapter 3. The world can be quite disorienting, and it's often hard for our children and teens to know what they are looking at and how to engage with it. Whether it is something deadly serious, such as a terrorist attack, or something fun, such as karaoke singing at church, over and over again our children need us to frame what is happening, where they can find God and how they can respond.

God and his truth are woven into all our experiences in life. Don't feel the need to cram information into your child; just be aware of where your child may need some explanations and take the opportunity to provide those, describing what the experience means *to you*. Worry less about saying the right thing and free yourself more to say, 'When I see this or do this, it's because I believe…'

Framing is essential in helping our children understand who God is in the world and how to engage with him. And God has placed us, *as parents*, into our children's lives to walk alongside them throughout their normal daily lives to show them where he is. If you want to re-explore this tool, you can refresh yourself and see more examples on page 47.

3 Unwinding

We are all on the journey of understanding God. Our view of God is continually shaped as we go through life, read scripture and are influenced by others. It is the same for our children. As they hear stories of scripture, see and interact with the world around them and get to know those who love God, our children develop an understanding of God that grows with them. But as with all people, that view can become warped, unbalanced or tangled up. Our children may begin to feel that God is distant and disconnected from their lives or that God is only interested in happiness and gets annoyed at those who don't find Christian joy quickly. They may become fixated on the wrath of God and begin to think that God is generally angry and looking to punish them. They may swing one way and think God is mysterious and chaotic, and then swing the other way and think he is little more than their everlasting buddy. As they go through life, their experiences, thoughts and learning continue to shape how they view God, and how they view God significantly impacts how they choose to engage with him.

It's our privilege as parents to be so embedded in those insignificant moments of our children's day that we can notice and capture how their view of God is developing and impacting their faith journeys. Then, when needed, we can nudge them back towards a more balanced and accurate direction. We can unwind any confusion or mixed messages that our children begin to believe about God. This isn't about teaching our children more or telling them they are wrong; it's about noticing what has begun to warp their view of God and enabling them to talk about it and wrestle with it. It may mean exposing them to broader ideas of God's character or noticing when we are feeding into that warped view. It may mean asking open-ended questions or enabling them to talk through difficult concepts. As parents we can do this, because it is usually in those ordinary moments and conversations that we notice what our children's perception of God is, and so we can also in those moments begin to correct their unhealthy views of God. When we enable our children to talk openly about their thoughts on God, we enable them to explore and find him.

As church leaders, our children can often feel the pressure to perform for us and others, and so they can be very attached to the 'right answers' that will please us. When we ask open-ended questions, like 'If you went back in time and could see one Bible story live, what would it be?', we empower our children to genuinely talk about how they view God and scripture and how they feel about it all. If we steward these conversations well, listening carefully, affirming how we see their point of view and occasionally sharing ours, we will be empowering them to walk their faith journey together with us, rather than perform it for us.

As you gain insight into how your children view God, you can casually begin to use the other Key Tools – creating windows into your journey of understanding God and framing key situations and ideas for them, so that you can encourage and help shape their developing view of God.

4 Chat and Catch

Another Key Tool that parents are wonderfully positioned to use is Chat and Catch. It can be so easy for church leaders' children, in particular, to struggle with prayer. Everyone is on a prayer journey, and it is easy for prayer to become formulaic or seem to be a burden for children. We know, of course, that prayer is an essential part of life with God, and so it can be excruciating as parents to watch our children struggle with it.

In my experience of ministry with children and teens, I have found that the formulas we have created to help children know what to say to God have often ended up creating in our children a sense of performance prayer. Children have no other relationships in their lives where they need to think through what they are going to say, before they approach the person and say it. That isn't how they talk to us or to their friends or siblings. And yet, often that is how we 'help' them to pray. Chat and Catch is a way of removing the barriers for children, so they can engage in authentic, conversational prayer, holding nothing back.

Chatting is simply enabling children to say what they want to God and to say it in the way they want. It's releasing them from the constraints of talking to him about 'thank you, sorry and please', and freeing them to simply say what is on their heart to God. While the natural progress of any relationship includes thanking, apologising and asking, it's not the *centre*. The centre of relationship is sharing fears and worries, laughing together, talking about hopes and dreams, and debriefing our days together. Chat enables our children and teens to share with God in that way.

Catching from God helps our children become aware of all the wonderful ways God communicates with us. In the Bible, God has shown us that he communicates with people in many different ways. Our children can grow to expect that they will learn to recognise his voice, his communications, just as he has promised they would. By talking with our children about all the different ways God communicates, we can raise our children's expectations that as they talk with him, he is proactively communicating with them. We all need God's guidance, truth, love and assurance in our lives. When we proactively help our children look for what God is saying to them and for what that looks like in their lives, then we free them to live in conversational prayer with God.

If you want to explore this more, I'd encourage you to read *Parenting Children for a Life of Faith* (BRF, 2018) or view the free Parenting for Faith course at **parentingforfaith.org**. Both resources go into exercises to help you introduce these concepts to your children.

How we parent for faith at home is absolutely central to how our children will grow to know God. Being around the church isn't enough. God designed children and teens' discipleship to be rooted in the ordinary, mundane bits of life, and you as a parent are perfectly positioned to use these Key Tools to help your children build a life with God now and into their future.

5 Surfing the Waves

A lot of parenting for faith is proactive, but it doesn't always have to be planned. The final Key Tool is called Surfing the Waves. We know that God is active in the lives of our children. They are human beings with waves of interests and waves of growing in God. As they develop, they also experience waves of emotional and mental growth. If we can learn to surf the waves of their lives with them, then we can facilitate and encourage whatever is happening in their lives and help them find God in it. To surf the waves of our children's spiritual lives, we need to learn a few principles of actual surfing.

1 *Identify the waves* – A novice surfer sees merely that there are waves coming; an experienced surfer sees the waves, but also judges from afar which waves are worth catching and why, based on their size, colour, shape, speed and so on. Too often we think that the only spiritual opportunity we have to speak to our children about God is when they ask a deep theological question. But we have opportunities through their natural interests, their curiosity in something, what makes them angry, the stories they play out and the random ideas they want to enact. Any of these things can present a spiritual wave to jump on board.

2 *Not every wave is your wave* – Surfers spend ages sitting in the ocean looking for waves to ride. Some waves aren't big enough or are too fast. Some are the wrong shape or are angled in the wrong direction. Others look perfect, but the surfer is not positioned in the right place to catch them. Whatever the reason, waves come and go, and surfers can't jump on every one. They just catch the

ones that feel right. In our children's spiritual lives, there will be opportunities we will miss or can't jump on. That is okay. Don't spend time wishing for waves you can't catch; just look for the ones you can.

3   *Paddle at the right speed* – To catch a wave, surfers have to paddle at the same speed as the wave. Paddle too slowly and they will miss it; too quickly and they aren't surfing. Once we see a wave rising in our children's spiritual lives, our job is to paddle alongside them and be ready to surf the spiritual wave *with* them at *their* pace. We can get excited and try to jump ahead and lead them in surfing the wave, but that usually results in us not surfing the wave well. We can miss a wave by trying to take it over and control it: 'You want to read the Bible? Great! Let's do a family devotional every day and memorise scripture and have a one-year Bible-reading plan.' Or we can miss a wave when we are so afraid that we just raise our eyebrows and don't say anything. Both ways, the wave can pass. But when we learn to go at *their* pace, asking a question and offering help for the next step, we can facilitate a fantastic wave in our children's lives.

4   *The wave lasts as long as it lasts* – Surfers can ride a wave for five seconds, 15 seconds or for what seems like forever. Sometimes the wave looks like it will last a long time, but then it suddenly breaks on top of the surfer. Because waves can be unpredictable in their length and strength, surfers try to ride each one for only as long as they can. And when the ride is over, they paddle back out and wait for the next wave that is just right for them.

The waves of our children's lives are similar. Some spiritual waves may look great, but then they can collapse quickly. Our child may be passionate about mission, but by the time we've bought a biography of a famous missionary in the country she is interested in, she has decided that she isn't interested at all. Other waves may last longer than we think, and for months our children will be asking a thousand questions at bedtime, wanting to hear the same CD over and over or listening again and again to the same worship song.

It's worth staying with the waves, even if they try your patience. The moment is *now*, so ride the waves and follow your children's lead. It may mean you need to sacrifice more of your time, but it will be worth it.

All waves break eventually. Be prepared to let them go gracefully. We've all had the experience of trying to continue with something that our kid doesn't want to do. This isn't homework; it's their wave. When you see the wave begin to peter out, bail out before it breaks. It's okay. Don't be disappointed or worry that they are backsliding. There will be another wave.

15

Coaching our children in how they engage with church

I can't remember one particular moment when I first discovered that I loved the church. I think the feeling crept up on me over time. I remember as a child having that sense of belonging to a church community and feeling needed. I loved doing anything that required my sheer force of strength and effort. If there was a physical task to do, I was there, alongside a bunch of other people of all ages, grunting and sweating as we lifted chairs and rolled tables. I loved the power a team had when everyone came together, and I loved being valued and needed as a part of it.

I remember as a university student being a member of my parents' Bible study group at church. I saw the richness of a diverse community of people studying the Bible together, listening to each other's wisdom and insights, and genuinely praying for each other's families and work situations. I understood the deep provision of challenge and support that the community church group provided.

I remember as a young adult being part of a church staff team for the first time, and seeing the impact a team could have upon the local community as we served together. I learned how important it was to do the work we did. I loved seeing lives changed by God, and I loved being a part of the transformation he was bringing to individuals, families and our town.

Little by little, I grew to love God's church, and I knew I wanted to serve it.

What was your journey of growing to value and love the church? What made you choose to say, 'I am willing to give myself to the service of God within the church'? Whatever our paths, we have all ended up holding close to our hearts this beautiful, messy thing called the church.

When we value something, we want our children to value it too. We want our children to see and love the church, not just tolerate it. We want our children to truly *engage* and connect with our church, because it is a family of God who will love and encourage them. It is a community who will support and inspire them to know and love God and help them grow in connection with him. Church is more than just a service to attend; it is a deep and powerful blessing God has given us all, and we want our children to experience that.

We don't want their status as 'church leader's child' to rob them of the importance, power and blessing of their broader status as 'congregation member'.

So how can we help our children grow in their love of the church and learn how to engage with it to the fullest?

Experiencing the British Museum

One of my favourite places in the world is the British Museum in London. The building itself is gorgeous, especially the great court with its gleaming white walls and glass ceiling. I love just sitting there, watching people mill around and hearing the sound of different languages. I love the murmurings in the central library room and the smell of dry, old books stacked up to the heights. I love walking through rooms full of history, seeing ancient everyday artefacts and works of artistic creativity. I can't help but smile as I walk past people calling each other over to point out what they've just discovered or to share what they've just learned. I am thrilled when a docent gives a demonstration and invites me to touch objects from the past: a coin from China in 342BC or a figurine from Ancient Mesopotamia. There is so much to love about the museum.

One time I was in the British Museum taking a break between meetings, and a school group arrived for a short trip to see Egyptian artefacts. The teachers and volunteer parents had the children in lines and conducted them with lightning speed through the gorgeous atrium. When several children slowed down to gasp at the beautiful space, a parent intervened with a quick, 'Don't stop to ogle. Keep moving!' and then shuffled them back to their place in line. It wasn't long before another two children spotted some African figurines through a side door and with overwhelming joy started running towards them, only to be caught by another observant parent who directed them back to the group.

I watched the students as they entered the Egyptian rooms and were dispersed to explore the exhibits. Some loved the place immediately, but others were quickly bored and restless. The bored and restless ones struggled to stay focused, and the leaders continually encouraged them to finish their papers and complete their tasks. As the children passed me by, some of the ones who had been swept away by the grand architecture of the entrance or the African figurines were now commenting how boring the museum was.

I was so frustrated. The museum is more than just a few statues to see. It's the environment, the sensory experience, the history, the creativity, the community of learning. It's a place where everyone can find something intriguing and relevant to their current interests or their past, and everyone can be fascinated and challenged by being exposed to something different. And yet, for most of these children on this specific trip, they missed all that. Their experience was completely focused on the task at hand: the time-limited group activity assigned to them. They visited the British Museum, but they didn't truly experience it.

So often, our children's experience of church can be similar to this. Life gets busy, and our concept of 'helping our children engage with church' easily slips into 'helping our children do all of the activities in the church service without complaining' or 'helping our children participate in their midweek groups'. We can accidentally become overly focused on the activity at hand and miss the endless beauty and opportunities of the wider church experience.

We are in the beautiful position of helping our children navigate through the different aspects of church without leading them like those students in the museum. Rather, we can help them learn to engage with the church in their own way, pursue their own varied interests in their own time and cherish the areas of church they choose to explore. So let's look at what those areas are and how we can help our children experience and grow in them all.

Different areas of church

We have so many aspects of church that we treasure! If we were to fully explore the wonder of the church, we could fill an entire book with our findings. So, to make it easier to consider some of the significant areas of church, let's narrow our focus to a few. Feel free to choose other areas or to add your own to this list; the point is that our children need to experience and learn how to engage with the many areas within the church. Once we have identified these areas, then we can begin to help our children engage with them proactively. I would suggest these aspects as a start:

- *Drawing near to God (Hebrews 10:19–24; Acts 2)* – The church is a place to wholeheartedly encounter God through worship, preaching, kids' groups and prayer times. We want our children to meet with God through the community and activities of the people in our church.

- *Radically loving others (John 13:34–35; Acts 2)* – The church is a place to radically love and encourage others, and to receive that love and encouragement in return. We want our children to sacrificially and joyfully put down their lives for each other, to live full of compassion and love and to draw alongside other people on their journey. We want them to receive all of that from the community as well.

- *Spurring each other into action (Hebrews 10:23–25; Mark 16:15–20; Acts 11:19–30)* – The church exists in part to enable Christians to challenge and support each other, to wrestle with scripture together and share their tough questions, and to be part of a group that encourages and equips each other to live a life honouring God and what he has called each one of us to do.

- *Giving each part a purpose (1 Corinthians 12:12—13:13; Ephesians 4:11–16)* – The church is a place where every person is a purposeful part of the body of Christ and is needed by the whole church, and where we can all value the contributions of others. We want our children to see that they are valuable, unique and useful in the greater calling that God has for his church.

- *Pursuing the Spirit (Galatians 5:16–26; Acts 2)* – The church is a place to pursue and experience the work of the Spirit, both in the internal transformation of becoming more like Jesus and in participating in his active work in the world.

When we begin to reflect on these aspects of church, we can then assess how our children are engaging with them in the fullness of church, and we can create new ways to enable our children to experience them. For us to do so, we need to grow in our own confidence of proactively helping our children grasp these values. One method we can use is called the six-stage circle.

The six-stage circle

This method makes use of skills you *already have* to help you proactively disciple your children in an intuitive way. You will notice that the six stages follow a natural progression of coaching that you *already use* in one way or another as parents. These are the stages:

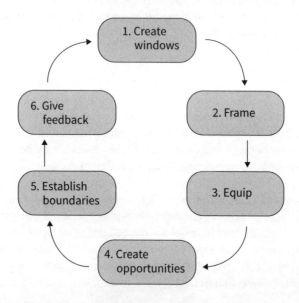

Here is an example of how natural it is to use the six-stage circle. I have a friend who loves board games – I mean *loves* board games. His kids, though, just merely enjoyed board games, until their dad unconsciously discipled his children into loving board games through this process.

- He *created windows* into how much he loved board games. It oozed out of him. He joined Facebook groups and bought and sold games. He traded them online and researched new ones. He talked about them a lot, and when a new game arrived at his house, his glee was contagious.

- With every new game he set up, he *framed* for his children why that game was unique or different and how it was to be played. Together he and his children analysed the game's format, what strategies were best to use and which rules helped or didn't help. They talked about what they liked or didn't like about the game and how they would improve it. They took the conversation a step further and discussed the generalities of games: what made a good game and how many different categories of games were on the market.

- He also began *equipping* them to love games. He bought games at different difficulty levels, so that his 4-year-old and 12-year-old could love games that were challenging and hilarious to each of them. When one of his children expressed a desire to create her own game, my friend helped her collect supplies and gave her a space to work. As she progressed, she experimented with rules and game pieces. My friend would leap in with encouragement and commitment and play her prototype with her, asking her questions to help her refine her thoughts about her rules and the mechanisms she needed to make her game work as she had envisioned.

- He *created opportunities* for his children to experience games, both at home and in big arenas. He organised a day trip hours away to the national games expo, and they giggled their way through the day testing games that hadn't been released yet, talking to designers, trading games and agonising over buying new ones. The kids brought their own money, and they all hunted down what they wanted and debated what would be good to buy and what wouldn't.

- This father light-heartedly *established boundaries*, making sure the children protected their games and counted all the pieces in and out. He didn't want them to waste their money on games they might not like, so he enabled them to research reviews and compare prices before they made a decision.

- He gave his children fantastic *feedback* by practically glowing whenever he played games with them, laughing and enjoying each game, from the simplest to the most complex. As a result, their connection times together were filled with support, encouragement and a real sense of team and family. And the children developed a deep *love* for games.

As you can see, we as parents naturally utilise these stages as we encourage and enable our children to thrive in new areas of their lives. We can do the same when it comes to areas of their faith. We can take a core value or belief and work it around the circle by applying the six stages in the intuitive order. It doesn't require a lot of time or effort, just a choice.

The problem is that with faith, we often miss out on working around the *complete* circle. We tend to default to using just two stages: create windows ('See what I do? Okay, now you do it!') and establish boundaries ('In this family, we go to church!'). When we do that, we are only enforcing religious activity. When we skip over frame, equip, create opportunities and give feedback, our children miss out on the stages in which they will learn, grow, acquire confidence and finally own the core value. If we want to truly disciple our children in their relationship with God, we need to coach them through all the stages.

Using the six-stage circle to disciple our children

The joy of already knowing the areas of the church we value is that we will never feel trapped in finding a place for our children to explore spiritually. If our children are struggling with the service, we don't need to double down on forcing them to like it. They may simply be ready to explore a different area of church, and we can help them take that next step in their exploration. Maybe we have been pushing them to draw near to God in the service, but their next step may be to dig into loving others and feeling loved by them. Or if they are burning out with all the hospitality required of them, then it may be time to enable them to find their own purpose within the church community. As we disciple our children through their new explorations, we can use the six-stage circle.

Let's look at two examples of how to use the six-stage circle to help our children explore two specific values of the church: drawing near to God and spurring each other into action. Remember, you are the experts in your children, so only you will know how these six stages will play out best for them. These are merely examples to illustrate two possibilities.

Using the six-stage circle: drawing near to God

- *Create windows* – Often in church we're trying to balance a thousand things: keeping our eye on the projections that change too slowly, watching the drunk homeless man who has wandered in and is starting to cause a problem, sorting out the last-minute gluten-free Communion wafers, wrangling our children and making notes on the notices. But one of the most powerful things we can do *for* our children is to genuinely worship in front of them, whatever that looks like. Whether you raise your hands, sing loudly or stay silent, create a window for them to see you drawing near to God during that time. You would be amazed at how often church leaders' children never see their parents authentically and wholeheartedly engaging with God at church. If you can't do that at your church, you may want to consider how you can create those times in other places or ways. If we want to be leaders who say to the parents in our congregations, 'It is important for your kids to see you worship,' then we need to find ways to do it ourselves too.

- *Frame* – Our children may not yet understand how to connect with God in worship. If they don't, you could take the opportunity to whisper, 'Look, can you see how the different types of people are worshipping in different ways? What do you think is going on in that person's heart? And that person's?' Whatever aspects of worship are important to you, frame them for your children so they can fully understand the words and behaviours used in the worship time.

- *Equip* – Our children may need help engaging in the worship. If they don't know all the words to a song, find the track online so they can become familiar with it. If they can't see the words, move them forwards. If you need to explain every song so that they understand what the words mean, do so. In whatever way you need to equip them to fully participate in worship, go for it.

  Our children may also need to be equipped to proactively decide what type of worship works for them. One church leader's teenager told me that he loves worshipping at home alone but hates worshipping at church with his family in the front row because he feels like everyone is watching him. He said his parent told him that he could feel free to move to whatever spot works best for him. They said that having a place to comfortably worship was more important than sitting together as a family. So now, when the worship happens, he just slips out and sits on the floor behind the pews to worship without being seen. That has significantly changed the way he feels about worship in church.

- *Create opportunities* – If we want our children to value something, they need to have the opportunities to explore it. The more opportunities they have to find their own comfortableness in worship, the more they will value it. We can help our children explore drawing near to God by keeping them in church for the worship so they can become comfortable with it. Sometimes when church leaders' children grow into teenagers, they struggle to worship around people who have expectations of them, so some church leaders create opportunities for their teen to attend a different church in the evenings. One family I know went to an evening service together at a different church so they could have the opportunity to worship side by side. Another family

I know faced a tough decision when their child wanted to attend a different church's youth group. Whatever you decide, your journey is to proactively explore for yourself and with your children the opportunities for drawing near to God in worship.

- *Establish boundaries* – Feel free to create boundaries. You can say, 'This is our time to draw near to God, and because of that I don't want you to play on any gadgets,' or, 'This is the time we draw near to God. How do you want to do it? You can do it in all of these ways; you can't do it in these ways. What do you want to do?' This is an important aspect of empowering our children to find their own paths. Rather than dictating what their behaviour should be, we can say to them, 'You have vast freedom within this boundary.'

- *Give feedback* – Spend time after church talking with your children about their experience of drawing near to God in the worship and why it was like that. Whether or not it was a great time of worship, you can talk about what got in the way or what made the experience particularly special. Whatever it was, share your journeys of faith with each other.

Whether it's in worship, prayer or engaging with scripture, by helping our children explore the value of drawing near to God during services and midweek groups, we can empower them to find him near in every context.

Using the six-stage circle: spurring each other into action

- *Create windows* – If we want our children to experience the wonderful challenge and encouragement of being part of the church, we can begin by creating windows into what it means to spur on others in the faith and to have others spur us on in our own faith and journey. Let your child see you listening to other people's sermons and to other members' wisdom and insights about God and scripture. Talk about how an experience with God or scripture changed you or shaped you, or how a friend challenged you theologically or personally.

- *Frame* – Frame for your child how one part of being church is being vulnerable enough to share what we are feeling and thinking, and being open to receiving the encouragement and challenges of the community around us. When someone in your congregation encourages you in person or through email, share it with your family and tell them how it strengthened or excited you to continue in your efforts.

- *Equip* – As children and teens grow, they learn how to spur people on – how to encourage without forcing and how to challenge without crushing. Sometimes they need to practise this skill in their families. Take a few minutes to describe how 'spurring each other on' works: we can remind people of forgotten truth, speak courage when people have lost hope or cheer people on when they get tired and want to give up. When we notice our children trying this at home, give feedback, such as 'What a great encouragement. I feel like I can do this now,' or, 'I love how when your brother thought he couldn't do his homework, you reminded him of times when he persevered and succeeded. Thank you for encouraging him.'

- *Create opportunities* – Life is full of opportunities to invite our children to spur us and others on to good works and faith. When you are feeling discouraged, feel free to share a bit with your children and tell them you need some spurring on. You can say, 'I need some strengthening words right now. Can you encourage me?', or, 'I need some wisdom on this sermon. It keeps coming out wrong.' When we create opportunities for our children to encourage us and spur us on, we need to make sure we feed back well so they can see the change. We can also begin to look around as a family and come up with plans to spur others on. Who is doing a project that needs encouragement and help? What could we do to jump on board and strengthen and encourage others in what God has called them to do?

- *Establish boundaries* – We can set boundaries so our children understand the power behind the value. We can say, 'The ability to encourage and motivate each other is a really powerful gift because our words and actions are powerful. And because we know they are so powerful, we are very careful in our family to use our words to bring support, kindness and encouragement to each other. That's why there are consequences for… We take this seriously.'

- *Give feedback* – Help your children see the impact of their acts of spurring others on. Show them how things couldn't have been done without them, how their words blessed people and how their actions enabled others' callings. Show them the powerful effect people can have in the world when they spur each other on.

Remember, no matter what your children are feeling about church, they can always take the next step into a new area of exploration within the church. If drawing near to God seems to be causing a struggle, then suggest they focus on something else. They may be ready to just embrace the community of church and find significance in that. Or they may be ready to wrestle with the sharpening aspects of learning and being part of a challenging team. Remind yourself of all the different values of church you treasure. There is never a dead end – just more of church to explore.

Remind yourself of all the reasons you love the church, and help your children discover them all. Don't worry if they are struggling with one value of the church. Within all the values we talked about – drawing near to God, radically loving others, spurring each other into action, giving each part a purpose and pursuing the Spirit – our children have plenty of space to grow and connect with the church.

16

Tricky bits: building our children into the body of Christ

Because of our influence and positioning as church leaders, we have great opportunity within our church to help our children stretch their wings and explore their part in the body of Christ. How can we empower our children in ways that will help them thrive in ministry rather than be buried under work or obligation?

Here are things to consider as we empower our children in ministry.

Start with their passion

Most children, at some point, help their parents with various aspects of their job. My mother, for example, was an English teacher, so I spent many hours before and after school grading spelling tests, cutting out craft items and helping with display boards. My father was a police officer, so my childhood included role-playing as a criminal when he ran scenarios at the police academy and participating in drug demonstrations at local secondary schools. We all help our parents at some point, and that is part of the joy of being a kid.

It is also common for church leaders' children to help out their parents, particularly when they work in smaller churches. We ask our children to step into roles that no one else seems to want or into the holes in the rota. I have heard many stories of children being the sole welcomer at church and of teens running children's groups, leading the singing or playing the piano because that was what their parents needed them to do.

While having our children help us can be a part of normal family life, we need to keep in mind that as church leaders we want every member of our church to be fulfilling their part of the body of Christ, including our children. If we want our children to grow and discover what part they can play in church and community, we need to be empowering them to find what they feel *called* to do, rather than narrowing their options to what we *ask* them to do.

We can start by helping our children identify what they are passionate about, not just what they are good at. We are all on a journey of saying 'yes' to what God asks us to do. Sometimes that is in line with our skills and giftings, and sometimes it isn't. Sometimes God asks us to do bold things that don't match what we are naturally good at; Moses, Gideon and Esther knew this from experience.

Part of belonging to a church is having the opportunity to explore ways of getting involved in what you are passionate about. If we limit our children to only what they are good at, we are focusing them on what they think they can bring, rather than what God is stirring inside them to do. Your daughter may play the piano, but maybe she is actually very passionate about developing the technology and sound equipment for the church. You may want to steer your son to the set-up team, but then he may miss out on discovering his much-needed skills of networking people and making them feel loved. You may ask your teens to lead in children's ministry because they have a lot of energy, when actually they want to read the Bible from the front and eventually preach.

We have lots of ways we can uncover our children's passions. Some-times our children will voice what they want to get involved in, and other times they need us to help them discover what they are passionate about. Ask them open-ended questions that get them talking about their thoughts and feelings about the church, such as:

- If you had £100,000 to spend on the church or church ministry, what would you do with it?
- If I put you in charge of church for one day, what would you do?
- If every adult got sick on the same morning and all the kids and teens had to lead the service, what would you want to do?
- What is one thing that puts people off church?

These and other open-ended questions can help get your child thinking and talking, and you can begin to discover what they might want to pour their energy and time into. Sometimes the place they want to be powerful in is the place they criticise most.

Be open to a wider view of your children's interests. A child who loves drama may not want to do drama in church. Their love of drama may actually be a comfortableness and confidence in front of a crowd, which may mean you have a skilled service leader in the making. Whatever you notice, help your children identify their passions and find ways they can respond to those passions within the church context and throughout their broader life.

If you want to explore this more, check out Part 2 of *Parenting Children for a Life of Faith*, omnibus edition (BRF, 2018). This is a whole section dedicated to helping our children know their purpose and learn to be bold about living it out in church and in their lives.

Treat them like a congregation member

Our children will benefit from being treated like every other member of the congregation. For us, that means we need to support and encourage them through the natural processes of volunteer selection and scheduling. If there are specific hoops people need to jump through to be on a team, ensure that your child jumps through those hoops, too. If there are requirements for quality or faithfulness, make sure your child is held to the same standard.

For example, let's say your 13-year-old son is keen to join the adult worship team. Your church's normal procedure may be to give people an audition and a six-week trial period. Your child, though, is very shy, and you know the audition process is putting him off joining the team. If you decide to use your position as church leader by talking to the worship leader and asking for a private audition or a shortened procedure, then you may be robbing your son of the opportunity to experience the full strength of his journey in choosing to be part of the body of Christ.

Since you understand that part of the necessity of an audition is to encourage people to face their fears and to want to join enough that they are willing to take a risk, it's important you respond first as a parent rather than as a church leader. As a parent, you know your son's weakness, so you can coach him into confidence to be ready for the audition. When he completes the audition process and trial period on his own, he will feel he belongs on the team and has earned his place. Giving our children the dignity of joining a team like everyone else and stepping into the full responsibility of the role hooks our children into feeling needed and valued as part of the body.

Give leaders permission to lead your children

Our congregation members love us and our children. Yet, for a variety of reasons, many congregation members feel awkward about having a church leader's child on their team. It could be they are worried that if the child doesn't like something, the church leader will overreact. Others know that because they have a soft spot, they will let the child get away with anything.

Congregations often don't know how to lead a church leader's child. They may need to hear specific encouragement and permission from us. We can say:

> Feel free to really lead my kid. He will make mistakes, flake out and need discipleship and encouragement like everyone else, and I think you are going to be a great leader for him. If my kid isn't fulfilling his role, please treat him with the same grace, firmness and challenge you would everyone else. And please grow him and create opportunities for him like everyone else. My kid needs people like you in his life, and I want him to really experience what it's like to be a part of the church.

Take it around the six-stage circle

Remember, helping our children find their place in the body of Christ is about coaching them in how they are needed as part of the church, and how they can respond to God's prompting in their lives. It's about being a servant of others. All the ideas you want to share with your child on this topic will have the biggest impact when you discuss them utilising the six-stage circle.

Create windows into your journey of how you found your place in ministry, and how your ministry and location have changed over the years. Share how you decide where to put your time and effort.

Frame for your children why it's important that they are a part of the church community, and why they are needed. Frame for them the impact others in the church have had on you and also the impact your children have had on others, so they can see their potential impact on others in the future.

Equip your children with any practical skills they need so they can be confident and competent in what they feel stirred to do. Children and teens need more equipping than we may think. Sometimes they need to learn basic skills: how to shake someone's hand, how to make others feel at ease, how to read loudly without yelling or how to hold a baby. Whatever they feel called to, give them the equipping they need to make a meaningful impact on others. This equipping is not to control or dictate how they minister, but to get them over the hindrances that hold them back. If we sense our children are struggling with us equipping them, we can step back and help them find others who can do so.

Create opportunities to explore how our children can get involved with their passions. Introduce them to the people who lead teams they want to join. If there are no teams to join, connect them with others who share their passion.

If you feel it is important that your children serve now, feel free to *establish boundaries* around their involvement. Only you will know what boundaries are appropriate for your family. Some families say, 'You have to be serving somewhere twice a month,' while others say, 'Find what you are passionate about and we'll discuss it, but I want you involved with the church and its ministries in some way.' You decide what boundaries you want to put on your children's involvement in ministry.

Lastly, make sure your children can see the impact they are having on others, and can hear the *feedback* of how others are blessed and changed by their willingness to serve.

FAQs

Deciding how to fit our family traditions in around a very busy Christmas ministry schedule is hard. How do we negotiate that in a way that helps my children feel connected and prioritised?

Christmas can be a hard time for church leader families, especially if you entered ministry when your children were old enough to remember life *before* you were a church leader. People take this approach in multiple ways. Some church leaders choose to put specific dates in their diary and then make them inviolable. I've known church leaders to say, 'We always do Christmas Eve breakfast together as a family, so I won't put anything in the church diary that would impinge upon that.' On the other hand, I've known church leaders who feel trapped by the church diary and say, 'We'll have to see how the church diary turns out and then we can see what our family Christmas will look like this year.' Every church context is different, and your ability to be flexible may change from location to location. What is important is that you as a family work together on what your Christmas will look like, rather than everyone feeling helpless.

Start with making sure that you are approaching this discussion from a place of connection. It's helpful to talk to your family about how this is an ongoing experiment: 'Last year we did it this way, and we felt really tired and not connected, so let's learn from that,' or, 'What do we love about how we as a family do Christmas and what worked great last year?' I've known families who took a few years to figure out that attending six services over Christmas Eve and Christmas Day robbed them of feeling like they'd had their family Christmas.

Each family solved it in different ways. One family decided to celebrate a family Christmas Eve and Christmas Day with all their traditions on 22–23 December. The dad took the days off, and they had a mini family holiday with energy and laughter, then they played with their toys and enjoyed the services while dad worked and then slept, exhausted, on Christmas Day.

For children to feel prioritised, they need to know that family life is a priority. How you choose to work that out can be different. Many church leaders have found it useful to establish a middle ground between flexibility and non-negotiable family time, and to be clear which is which. One family told me that they plan Christmas each year by making a list of their traditions – Christmas movie night with hot chocolate; going into town to see the lights; decorating Christmas cake – then, once the December church schedule has been set, they sit down as a family and plan their Christmas together, weaving their traditions into the work and school schedule. In this way, the children can see that it's everyone's schedule that has to be planned, rather than just saying, 'Let's not interfere with mum's job.'

Working together enables our children to feel powerful and able to respond to any stress or difficulty, because they aren't on their own complaining on the outside but rather part of the team who are committed to fulfilling everybody's desire for connection. It's about creating that culture of team where we as a family feel that together we are going to figure out how this best works for us.

How can I tell what is important to prioritise in my child's life?

Children and teens can find it hard to articulate well what is important to them. It is important to take into account children's feelings and priorities while also not restricting ourselves to them. Our children are complex individuals, so while we take on board and respond to the needs and feelings they are expressing, it is also our job to identify and input into their emotional and spiritual health and the connection between us, even if they don't express or identify that need. We make sure our children eat vegetables and brush their teeth. They aren't expressing that need, but we know it is healthy for them, so we make sure it happens. There will be times when your children or teenagers aren't expressing a need for connection or prioritisation. That doesn't mean they don't need it; it just means they may not know they have that need or how to express it.

I find that asking blunt questions can be helpful. This can be something as simple as, 'When I do X, does it make you feel disconnected?', or, 'What would you like me to do during X time?' These questions enable our children to explore what they feel, and we can help them share it.

For example, many church leaders' children have reported feeling very upset about their parents doing emails on their phone rather than actually watching when they are at activities such as swimming, gymnastics or martial arts. We all know how this goes. We take a child to their club and use that 20 minutes to get that last bit of sermon prep or emailing done. It's win–win, or so we think. The problem is that some children are making an enormous effort, or learning and failing, or accomplishing great challenges, and then they look up to see us missing it all for the sake of the church.

All it takes is a simple question: 'When I take you to swimming class, I usually use that time to do some work. I was wondering if that was disappointing or upsetting to you? If you could choose what I did during that time, what would you pick? Do you prefer I watch you, or do you not mind?'

Some kids want your face and smiles and encouragements, and others may not need it during that time at all. By keeping the flow of communication open, you can find out what they find important. I know some teens who genuinely don't look for connection at church, but are almost fanatical about making sure nothing interrupts their Thursday after-school ice-cream time. When we ask questions, we can find out what is most important for them.

A lot of what makes children feel unprioritised is the feeling of being squashed out, so when you are looking at how midweek meetings impact on bedtime or how a weekend away affects your time together, it can help to sit with your kids and say:

> This is a tricky one. Bedtimes are our best places to chat and catch up about our days. I love hearing about what you are feeling and thinking, and I'm not willing to stop that. But my work schedule is tricky this week. Can we figure out together when we can find those times? Keeping connected to you and your life is super important to me.

How you problem-solve will be as unique as your family. I know some church leaders who end all meetings at 9.15 pm so they can have time with their teenagers as they go to bed. Others start the bedtime routine before dinner so that they can read in bed at 5.00 pm, then the children go downstairs in their pyjamas to the dinner table. Others have an 'Ask me about' board where, if they don't get enough time together at bedtime, they make a list of things to chat about the next morning at breakfast. What matters is that we are creating space for children to voice and participate in making sure they are involved in an open and honest conversation with us about their feelings.

How does confidential information about the congregation negatively affect children or teens, so I can know what to look out for?

Our children *do* occasionally overhear confidential information about people in our congregations. Overhearing this confidential information can impact them in multiple ways. When we know how this impact tends to play out in our children's minds and hearts, we can proactively come alongside them and help coach them through their experience. I share these not to make us feel guilty, but so that we can be there to catch these effects when they happen and work to counteract them. Here are five common ways overhearing confidential information impacts children and teens:

1 When our children overhear our private conversations, they may think we are gossiping behind our congregations' back. They hear *how* we talk about others -- whether with a generous or critical view or with a concern for privacy or not – and hear how we as Christians and leaders care about those we serve. Hearing how we talk about others begins to shape our childrens view of how others in their congregations and their school may talk about them. It can grow in them a sense of others watching them and judging them.

2 When church leaders' kids overhear confidential pastoral information or details of internal church conflict, they become confused. They struggle to put the pieces into an understandable context. Because their brains are still maturing, and their life experiences are still new and few, children tend to see the world as black and white, and it can be hard for them to reconcile hearing many contrasting views or opinions about a person or a conflict.

For instance, your daughter may overhear that Mrs White doesn't want a baptistery in the new building and that it is making you frustrated. Yet she also knows that on Sunday Mrs White is nice to her. Your child may put these two facts together and conclude that Mrs White is a fake. Or your teen may overhear that Mr Blinkman and his wife are in counselling. Yet he sees that Mr Blinkman is on the worship team. Your teen may put two and two together and conclude that Mr Blinkman is making a big show of pretending to love God but is a hypocrite because he's in counselling, probably for something really big, like porn addiction.

When our children overhear pastoral information, they can develop a tainted view of us and those in our congregations. There may be sad consequences of this when the people we talk about are the very ones who are significant in the lives of our children. They may be the ones our children look up to and admire. They may be the families of their friends and the leaders whom they want to be like. They may be the older people who give them sweets or the university students who are beyond cool. And, of special importance, they may be the significant people who are in our children's 'sticky webs', the ones who are pouring out love and support on them. If we aren't careful, our children may discover confidential information that may impact how they think and feel about these heroes of theirs.

If you become aware that your children are struggling with this, they may need you to create some windows into how you see others with all their contradicting complexity – how you can be frustrated by Mrs White yet also grateful for all the support and encouragement she brings to you and others; or how you had counselling, and it was helpful to safely talk out loud to someone, so that you could process your emotions and be a better you, and so you are honoured to give other people space to hear God through it all.

3   When young children overhear our private conversations, they have no idea that what they've heard is confidential – after all, they *heard* it. To them, the facts are random bits of information they can offer out loud when they want to talk. It's important to remember that much of the time, our children's self-control mechanisms just aren't developed enough to remember what information to keep private. To keep confidential information private, they would first need to be able to juggle a complex set of variables: retain information about church plans or individuals, understand that it is confidential, remember who else knows the confidential information and pretend they don't know the rest of the time. Their brains are still developing, so don't be surprised when confidential information they know comes out in public. Most of the time, it isn't because they are wilfully disobeying or careless; it is because they are still developing the ability to handle that complexity.

If you become aware that your children are sharing confidential information, feel free to have a conversation about the value of protecting people's information, and how we only tell our stories not others'. But also be ready to be gracious and merciful, as our children will make mistakes as they grow and learn how to handle others' information.

4 When our children overhear church meetings in our home, they may misunderstand the contents and the context of those discussions. When they do, the knowledge may weigh heavily on them. One youth pastor told me how one day his church leader's teenage daughter came up to him with much emotion and cried, 'I heard my mum talking. She says that you might lose your job because there isn't enough money. I don't want you to go!' and then she ran away. The poor teen was buried under the worry and stress of coping with this new knowledge she thought she had, and she had agonised for a whole week before telling her youth pastor about it. It turned out she had overheard her mum working on the church budget with the budget committee and had completely misunderstood the conversation her mum was having. Our children can deeply own a problem they overhear.

It may be worth framing for your children that this may happen occasionally. You can simply say, 'Sometimes you may overhear information about the church that sounds worrying or confusing. If you do, feel free to ask me about it. You probably haven't heard the whole story, and I never want you to feel stressed or worried about anything you overhear. I won't be angry that you heard something.'

5 When our children and teens overhear confidential details about someone or the church, they may feel a burden of responsibility to do something with that information but feel powerless to do so. Be aware that they might struggle because they won't know how to help.

If we become aware of information our children hear, take the time to have a chat with them, explaining to them how things are being handled and assuring them that everything that can be done is being done. The goal is to remove that weight from their shoulders and heart, so they don't get buried under all the information with no way to influence or shape a response.

I think it's important to be authentic with my congregation and share information and stories about me, which includes my family life. How can I tell stories about me without exposing my children?

Many of us want to be the type of leader who is generous with ourselves and our personal stories, talking about our lives and history and encouraging others to do the same. Finding a balance between sharing our lives, which includes stories of our family, and still ensuring our family has the privacy they need can be incredibly difficult.

As parents, stories about our children and our family life are a part of what we want to share with those whom we want to get to know us. As church leaders, we want to tell stories about our family to our congregations as a way of creating windows into our lives and showing how our faith impacts how we do life. How do we engage in this process of being 'open and authentic' church leaders while also guarding our children's freedom and privacy?

While I still strongly advocate not telling stories in public that involve your children, there is a way of doing so in such a way that you are sharing *your* story, not *theirs*. Tell the story with you as the main character and with your thoughts and feelings as the main focus. Make all other details as private as possible.

For example, in a sermon or small group, as an illustration of dealing with a bad day, you may be tempted to tell a story like this:

> I was at the grocery store with the oldest of my three children, my son Alex, when he was three. Alex really struggled at that point with self-control. Like any normal three-year-old, when he wanted something, he wanted something. I remember once I had taken him to this same store, and, when I had my back turned for two seconds, he had somehow managed to grab a loaf of bread off the shelf, open it and stick his face into it like it was a feedbag. This kid had impulse-control issues. So this

time I was ready when we went to the shop. Lo and behold, we hit the cereal aisle, and he went ballistic. 'I want Frosties!' he was screaming. He was trying to get out of the trolley; it was like wrestling an alligator. Eventually, I had him trapped, and he was yelling, 'Help!' and a shop assistant offered to help. It was awful. He's much better now, but wow that was a bad day. Have you ever had a bad day when everything felt like it was falling apart?

This version of the story exposes the child to being laughed at by the whole congregation. If the whole point of your story is to help people identify with the feeling of having a bad day and who God is when you feel out of control, there is a way of telling that story well. You may have picked this story because you know that there are several parents in your congregation who are struggling and you really want to encourage them by being authentic, so you feel it's necessary to talk about parenting. If that's the case, then zero in on *your* experience of it. You could tell the same story, but with the focus on what you were feeling:

There are so many days in parenting when I feel like I'm utterly out of control and barely surviving. Has anyone ever done a grocery run with a toddler who has low impulse control? The screaming and the wriggling and the exhaustion. I remember on one occasion the situation was so loud I found myself surrounded by shop assistants, and I just wanted someone to hug me so I could cry out my shame of not being able to make this tiny person do what I wanted. I actually felt shame. You ever have one of those days?

Note that in the second story you were still able to talk about your parenting and your feelings, but you didn't name the child or give the specifics of the story.

I feel that God has called our family into ministry, not just me. How can I explain this to my children?

I find this question hard to answer because I believe it holds within it multiple desires for our children and multiple beliefs about calling and family. When some people ask this question, what they mean is:

- I don't want my children to feel powerless; I want them to feel that we are a team as a family.
- I want my children to feel considered and that God isn't only concerned about us as adults, but about them too. I want them to know that if God is calling us to this location and church, then he has good things for them there as well.
- I want my children to know that I see them as people able to contribute and help in this ministry and to use their skills and giftings as part of the body of Christ.

I am on board with all these values. I think they are fantastic. But then I would suggest that *those* are the statements and values to teach your children, rather than how God has called you as a family together. Create a conversation about those values: talk about being a team, and show them what that means in everyday ministry life. Talk about God weaving all things together for good, and create windows that reveal how he has led you and them and given you all good things in the past. Talk about what they bring to others, how God uses them wherever they are and how excited you are to see how God will work through them in the church.

When we insist on the language of 'calling', we are training our children in what that word means and how to respond to it. When we as church leaders decided we were 'called' into church ministry, it was a very personal journey of discernment, soul searching and choice. No one just marched up to us, informed us that we were called to church ministry and then required us to agree. We had to put in the effort of seeking out God's will and, once we knew deep down that God was calling us, make the choice to say yes.

If you are one of those church leaders who truly means that 'God has called my family into ministry, not just me', I suggest that the next step in explaining this to your children is to enable them to participate in a discernment process, appropriate for their age. Share stories of how you knew what God was putting before you, and tell them that God has great adventures and jobs for them to do. Talk about what they love, and help them find their place within the church. Talk about what you as a family are good at, and pray together about special jobs that God has for you as a family. If there is a move coming up, invite them into the discernment process, not necessarily for their consent but for their input and insight into what they feel is right for your family who ministers together.

What if my children don't like the children's groups or youth gatherings?

One of the pitfalls of being a church leader and a parent is that sometimes our children struggle with the church, and we try to problem-solve it as a church leader. If our child is struggling with the church or the children's or youth groups, then we can easily jump to thinking that the church needs to change. If our child felt unsafe during an event, then we can conclude that we need to fix the event. This can cause a lot of problems for you, your child and the teams that you lead for many reasons. The important principle to remember here is that we need to learn how to problem-solve *as a parent first*.

Your child is a unique individual, with their own quirks, spiritual journey and personality. If your child doesn't like an experience or is struggling in church groups, it doesn't mean that every child is having the same experience. It doesn't necessarily mean that the event or service is wrong. I have known many children's and youth ministries that have been forced to make adjustments and strategic choices based not on real wisdom and vision, but on the struggles of a church leader's child. Your child's experience, of course, is valid and true; just remember to problem-solve as a parent first.

If you weren't the church leader and your child was struggling to settle into children's ministry, you would have to problem-solve relationally. You would probably start by talking with your child about it and working to give them the tools to cope with their anxiety or disconnection and help them decide what to do next. In an extreme situation as an ordinary parent, we may quietly feed back to the leader, saying, 'It might not be everyone's experience, but Johnny seems to be struggling on a Sunday. He's a child who likes structure, and he tells me that when he arrives into the kids' ministry, he doesn't know where to go. Could you help me problem-solve how we can help him settle better?'

As the church leader, however, it is easy to think, 'That sounds very chaotic! If my kid is feeling that, then other children are feeling that. I'll call in our children's leaders to ask them about how children's ministry is running and tell them that they need to change the first part because chaos isn't welcoming to new people.' This reaction doesn't serve many people at all. It exposes our children and means that their leaders will stop treating them like every other child and see them as a whiner or troublemaker. It will give the impression that if the church leader's children aren't happy, then they as leaders will get in trouble. People may distance themselves from that kind of child.

It is also unfair to the leaders, who may have only had a really bad morning, are in the middle of a structural change or genuinely didn't notice that one child was struggling in a room of 25 happy ones. It also impacts on how your team trusts your wisdom, because they may be worried it is unduly influenced by your overfocus on your children. When we give direction, we want people to heed our counsel, not dismiss us.

Your child needs to know that when they struggle, you are responding to their need as a child, not seeing their personal struggle as an inside informant. Our children need to feel that we are there to help them, sometimes by equipping them, sometimes by facilitating them and sometimes by speaking up for them. They need to know that we can be trusted with their struggles and will help them to find solutions, that we trust them and will stay out of the way when they want to solve the problem themselves. If our children think that every time they complain to us, we might confront leaders or change the church, it makes them feel like we have our church leader hat on when they really wanted to talk to their parent and have us as a parent help them.

It can also backfire and create in our children a false sense of their own importance. I've known children who have learned that 'I'm going to tell my dad' is a threat that they can throw around. So always problem-solve as a parent first.

I want my child to feel free to be themselves at church, and not have to pretend to always be okay. How can I help them know and feel comfortable to be themselves at church?

If we want our children to be free to be themselves at church, one of the most powerful things we can do is to create windows into us being ourselves at church. If we want our children to feel free to be an imperfect person at church, we need to show them that we are imperfect at church and are okay with it, that we make mistakes and can laugh about them. If we want our children to be free to be emotional and have others encourage and support them, we need to be confident to show our children that sometimes we have bad days and to show them how we invite others to encourage and support us.

Our children watch how vulnerable, joyful and genuine we are at church, and they see the difference between us at church and us at home. They look and learn how free they can be in both places. You are the gift to your children. If you want them to be free and comfortable, create windows into how you do it and frame for them why.

Doesn't every parent need to know this stuff about empowering their children's journey with God? How can I help all the parents in my congregation with this?

Helping our children meet and know God is one of the greatest joys as parents that we get, and I want every parent to experience that for themselves. We at Parenting for Faith have created an enormous number of resources to help you create a culture of every parent growing to be confident to coach their children in their journey with God. Our website **parentingforfaith.org** hosts a lot of our resources, including:

- a free video-based Parenting for Faith course, which includes eight sessions and participant's and leader's guides (a DVD and printed guides are also available for purchase);

- a free fortnightly 20-minute podcast for parents;

- free access to over 200 videos and articles equipping parents on everything from spiritually helping children who are afraid of the dark to examples of how to help teens connect with God;

- church resources for church leaders as well as children's and youth leaders on how to create a culture that enables parents to flourish as spiritual parents;

- links to training days, conferences and our qualification in Parenting for Faith;

- links to books that can help, including *It Takes a Church to Raise a Parent: Creating a culture where parenting for faith can flourish* (BRF, 2018), which covers how to individually support parents as well as how we can hone our church structures to encourage and equip parents; and *Parenting Children for a Life of Faith: Helping children meet and know God*, omnibus edition (BRF, 2018), which empowers parents to help their children know God, pray freely, deal with struggles, find their purpose in life now and in the future, and build a God-centred core of confidence so they aren't knocked by the world's influence.

Parenting for Faith exists to help and equip you as parents and leaders. Get in touch and tell us how we can encourage and support you!

Notes

1 The Barna Group did a survey in the US called 'Prodigal pastor's kids – fact or fiction' and found that 33% of church leaders' children aged 15 and over were no longer actively involved in church, and 7% no longer considered themselves Christians. Compare this to the study released in the UK which states that 50% of the general population of children raised in church are no longer active in church as adults, and we can see that church leaders' children already have a better chance of sticking in church. The Barna Group also looked into the causes of church leaders' children choosing to walk away from church and faith, and found that parenting approaches influenced most of those reasons.

2 For a selection of the research, see the Bibliography on page 181.

3 Care for the Family, 'Faith in our families: a research report from Care for the Family', **careforthefamily.org.uk/wp-content/uploads/2014/08/Faith-in-our-Families-Research-booklet-Mar-2018-FINAL.pdf**.

4 M. H. Weber, 'Denominational attrition among adult children of Seventh-Day Adventist clergy', doctoral dissertation, Carey Theological College, Vancouver, British Columbia, 2008.

5 Kara Powell and Steven Argue, *Growing With: Every parent's guide to helping teenagers and young adults thrive in their faith, family, and future* (Baker Books, 2019).

6 Gary Chapman and Ross Campbell, *The 5 Love Languages of Your Family* (Northfield Publishing, 2009).

7 Weber, 'Denominational attrition among adult children of Seventh-Day Adventist clergy'.

8 See **parentingforfaith.org/PACL**.

9 Rachel Stevens and Matthew Stevens, 'Doing ministry together: life in an Australian clergy family', 2015, **australianclergyfamilies.com/publications**.

10 David Allen, *Getting Things Done: The art of stress-free productivity* (Viking, 2001).

11   Manoush Zomorodi, *Bored and Brilliant: How time spent doing nothing changes everything* (St Martin's, 2017).

12   John Larsson, *Those Incredible Booths: William and Catherine Booth as parents and the life stories of their eight children* (Salvation Books, 2015).

13   Kara Powell and Chap Clark, *Sticky Faith: Everyday ideas to build lasting faith in your kids* (Zondervan, 2011).

14   Weber, 'Denominational attrition among adult children of Seventh-Day Adventist clergy'.

15   This is one of the main reasons I started Parenting for Faith. As someone involved in church leadership, I wanted to invest significant time equipping parents and others to use their 2,000–3,000 hours a year to parent for eternal impact. If you want to know more about that journey and how to equip parents in your congregation to help their kids, see Rachel Turner, *It Takes a Church to Raise a Parent* (BRF, 2018).

16   Parenting for Faith exists to help parents of all kinds to grow in skill and confidence to help their children know God in the everyday. The website **parentingforfaith.org** has hundreds of articles and videos to help you on your journey, as well as a free eight-session Parenting for Faith video course for you to use at your convenience either individually or as a group or church. There is also a fortnightly 20-minute podcast for parents to equip and encourage them as they parent for faith. Please feel free to link in to all the parenting resources.

Bibliography

Books

David Allen, *Getting Things Done: The art of stress-free productivity* (Viking, 2001).

Holly Catterton Allen (ed.), *Intergenerate: Transforming churches through intergenerational ministry* (Abilene Christian University Press, 2018).

Gary Chapman and Ross Campbell, *The 5 Love Languages of Your Family* (Northfield Publishing, 2009).

Nell Goddard, *Musings of a Clergy Child: Growing into a faith of my own* (BRF, 2017).

John Larsson, *Those Incredible Booths: William and Catherine Booth as parents and the life stories of their eight children* (Salvation Books, 2015).

Rob Litzinger, *Pastor's Kid: The tragedy and triumph of growing up as a pastor's kid* (Rob Litzinger, 2011).

Barnabas Piper, *The Pastor's Kid: Finding your own faith and identity* (David C. Cook, 2014).

Kara Powell and Chap Clark, *Sticky Faith: Everyday ideas to build lasting faith in your kids* (Zondervan, 2011).

Kara Powell and Steven Argue, *Growing With: Every parent's guide to helping teenagers and young adults thrive in their faith, family, and future* (Baker Books, 2019).

Timothy L. Sanford, *'I have to be perfect' (and other parsonage heresies): The preacher's kid's manual of the holy heresies you may have grown up with and how to find your way back to the truth* (Llama Press, 1998).

Holly Tucker, *Serving God in the Fish Bowl: A 30-day devotional for pastors' kids* (Tate Publishing, 2016).

Rachel Turner, *Parenting Children for a Life of Faith: Helping children meet and know God*, omnibus edition (BRF, 2018).

Rachel Turner, *It Takes a Church to Raise a Parent: Creating a culture where parenting for faith can flourish* (BRF, 2018).

Manoush Zomorodi, *Bored and Brilliant: How time spent doing nothing changes everything* (St Martin's Press, 2007).

Research, articles, dissertations

Michelle E. Aulthouse, 'Clergy families: the helpless forgottens' cry for help answered through reality therapy', paper based on a program presented at the 2013 American Counseling Association Conference, 20–24 March, **counseling.org/docs/default-source/vistas/clergy-families-the-helpless-forgottens-cry-for-help.pdf?sfvrsn=1c17cd2b_11**.

Barna Group, 'Prodigal pastor kids: fact or fiction?', 11 November 2013, **barna.com/research/prodigal-pastor-kids-fact-or-fiction**.

Care for the Family, 'Faith in our families: a research report from Care for the Family', **careforthefamily.org.uk/wp-content/**

uploads/2014/08/Faith-in-our-Families-Research-booklet-Mar-2018-FINAL.pdf.

Bruce Hardy, 'Pastoral care with clergy children', *Review and Expositor* 98 (2001), **journals.sagepub.com/doi/abs/10.1177/003463730109800405**.

Lenore Johnson, 'Exploring the relationship between work, family and religion among clergy families', dissertation, Loyola University Chicago, 2010, **ecommons.luc.edu/luc_diss/271**.

Brian Jones, 'The clergy child: hidden in plain sight?', *Baptist Times*, 7 December 2016, **baptist.org.uk/Articles/484065/Clergy_children_hidden.aspx**.

Allen A. Lee, 'Ministry longevity, family contentment, and the male clergy family: A phenomenological study of the experience of ministry', dissertation, April 2017, Liberty University, **pdfs.semanticscholar.org/10b8/76d3507425e74f3d8339dbfd6fb3f9a0d436.pdf**.

Gail Murphy-Geiss, 'Clergy spouses and families in the United Methodist Church 2009 Part II: local church expectations and what clergy spouses most want the UMC to know', **gcsrw.org/Portals/13/SIte%20Migration/WhatClergySpousesWant.pdf**.

Rachel Stevens and Matthew Stevens, 'Doing ministry together: life in an Australian clergy family', 2015, **australianclergyfamilies.com/publications**.

Hijme Stoffels, '"Preachers' kids are the worst": results of a survey among clergy children in the Netherlands', paper presented at the annual meeting of the Association for the Sociology of Religion, San Francisco CA, 14 August 2004, **research.vu.nl/en/publications/preachers-kids-are-the-worst-results-of-a-survey-among-clergy-chi**.

Bonnie Studdiford, 'A resource guide to promote wellness within families of clergy', (FOCUS, 2006), **thewidowscorporation.org/uploads/files/FOCUS_ResGuide.pdf**.

Angela Tilby, 'Beware of Christmas family-olatry', *Church Times*, 9 December 2016, **churchtimes.co.uk/articles/2016/9-december/comment/columnists/beware-of-christmas-family-olatry**.

David Voas and Laura Watt, 'The church growth research programme: report on strands 1 and 2 – Numerical change in church attendance: national, local and individual factors', February 2014.

M. H. Weber, 'Denominational attrition among adult children of Seventh-Day Adventist clergy', doctoral dissertation, Carey Theological College, Vancouver, BC, 2008.

Book extract: Parenting Children for a Life of Faith

Nurturing children in the Christian faith is a privilege given to all of us whose responsibility it is to raise children. God's desire is that our parenting guides each child to meet and know him, and to live with him every day through to eternity.

In this fully updated compilation of her *Parenting Children for a Life of...* series, Rachel Turner explores how the home can become the primary place in which children are nurtured into

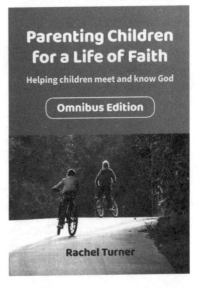

the reality of God's loving presence and are encouraged to grow in a two-way relationship with him that will last a lifetime. This book examines how we can enable our children to know what it means to be in a relationship with God, rather than just know about him – helping our children to be God-connected rather than merely God-smart.

The following is an extract from chapter 1 of the book.

1

Discipling proactively

In my experience, there is a big difference between a God-smart child and a God-connected one. I'm sure you have met both kinds of children in your life.

A God-smart kid knows the right Christian answers off the top of their head. They can pop off a lovely little prayer out loud, they know their memory verses and they often know more Bible stories than we do. They know the rules for Christian living and can easily slot into the rituals at church. They are comfortable with how to do Christianity, but it all seems to stop at their head.

A God-connected child, on the other hand, seems to have something extra, something that goes beyond head knowledge. A God-connected child lives in a vibrant two-way relationship with God. They share life with him, play with him and interact with him throughout the day. They know they are loved and handle the world with the confidence that comes from having the peace and healing of the living God in their daily reality. Their head knowledge of God is just a part of discovering a lifelong heart connection with him.

Our hearts long to create God-connected kids, but we can often feel trapped into only growing God-smart ones. We pour our effort into taking our children to church and teaching them about God and the Bible, and thereby hope that one day they'll wake up and be magically God-connected. It can make us feel like powerless spectators cheering on our children in their faith journeys. But that's not God's plan for us.

God's plan

God has a plan for how to create God-connected children, and it may come as a bit of a surprise.

> Listen, Israel! The Lord our God is the only true God! So love the Lord your God with all your heart, soul, and strength. Memorize his laws and tell them to your children over and over again. Talk about them all the time, whether you're at home or walking along the road or going to bed at night, or getting up in the morning. Write down copies and tie them to your wrists and foreheads to help you obey them. Write these laws on the door frames of your homes and on your town gates.
>
> DEUTERONOMY 6:4–9 (CEV)

It appears that God's plan for children to learn how to connect with him happens during the most boring parts of life. Look at the passage again. The prime time for our children to learn about God is in the most ordinary moments we have together: when we are at home in our pyjamas staring off into space while eating bran flakes; while we are wrapped up with each other on the couch all looking at our phones and tablets; during the eye-pokingly boring bus trips, or while walking to school; during the third kiss goodnight or the half-asleep cuddles in the morning; while we are getting dressed in a panic for church, or decorating our homes.

God designed children to learn how to connect with God in the mundane parts of our days because that is where he is. He is with us in every moment, loving us as we think and laugh and sleep. He is guiding us as we ponder and remember our days and consider what to do next. He is powerfully present as we shop and encounter others. If we want our children to know how to access God in everyday life, then it has to happen in everyday life – with us.

Church leaders have no access to those ordinary places with our families. Our children's church leaders don't wake up in our houses or go on the school run with us. They don't stand bored in a queue with us or watch our oldest kid at his swimming lesson while listening to our other child read. The church, it seems, isn't in places that God has designed for children's discipleship to happen.

We as parents, carers and members of extended families are perfectly positioned to help our children meet and know God. We spend on average between 2,000 and 3,000 hours a year with our children, whereas church only has 100 hours of all-together event time a year. The church isn't meant to be the centre of children's discipleship. It could never be as effective as we can be in the spiritual life of our children.

But that doesn't mean we are alone. In biblical times, when God instructed Moses on how children could find connection with him, parents were part of close-knit extended families. Those extended families were part of a wider clan, and those clans were part of a tribe of people. No parent was on their own. In modern times, we can often feel the loss of that community. Not all of us have a Christian extended family or community that supports us.

It is important that you know that the church is behind you, is for you, is cheering you on and is the community you can rely on. Other Christian parents will have your back, and there are people of all ages in your church who are willing to surround you, love you and help you on this journey. They can't do the job for you, but they can make sure you aren't doing it alone. And they can be the extended family of love and encouragement for you and your children. We as parents were never designed to be parenting for faith alone, and if you don't have that community around you, please link yourself into a church and let some people know that you need it.

To order a copy of Parenting Children for a Life of Faith –
omnibus edition by Rachel Turner (978 0 85746 694 5, £12.99)
go to **brfonline.org.uk**

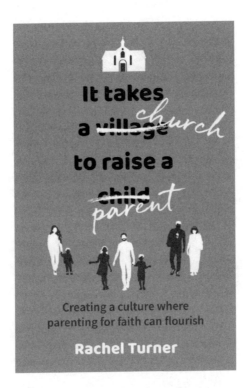

Creating a culture where
parenting for faith can flourish

Rachel Turner

Parents are the primary disciplers of their children, but we as a church are called to be their community who supports them as a family, equips them to succeed, and cheers them on the path of parenting for faith. This book will help children's, youth and senior leaders to learn how to position themselves for maximum impact, develop foundational values and practices to operate out of, and establish practical steps to shape a culture where parenting for faith can flourish.

It Takes a Church to Raise a Parent

Creating a culture where parenting for faith can flourish
Rachel Turner
978 0 85746 625 9 £8.99

brfonline.org.uk

Sleep, dreams and the night can be mysterious and sometimes troubling. Children can be afraid of the dark, have nightmares and night terrors, sleepwalk, or have insomnia. How do we deal with their concerns and fears and help them to draw close to God at night? This collection of Bible story retellings exploring God's character and promises will enable parents to help children grow in peace, confidence and understanding of who God is.

Comfort in the Darkness
Helping children draw close to God through biblical stories
of night-time and sleep
Rachel Turner
978 0 85746 423 1 £7.99

brfonline.org.uk

A comprehensive foundation for those working in the increasingly complex and diverse area of ministry with families, *The Essential Guide to Family Ministry* presents an overview of contemporary family life, sets out the principles that underpin this work and offers strategic and practical approaches to working with families. An essential read for all who are involved in this field and passionate about seeing God's kingdom come in families, churches and communities.

The Essential Guide to Family Ministry
A practical guide for church-based family workers
Gail Adcock
978 0 85746 578 8 £8.99

brfonline.org.uk

parenting for faith

Equipping parents to raise God-connected children and teens

Parenting for Faith inspires and equips parents to spiritually parent their children for faith, and resources churches to provide the supportive community that makes this possible.

Find out more at **parentingforfaith.org**

 brf.org.uk